The working parent's survival guide

The working parent's survival guide

Irene Pilia

WARD LOCK

A WARD LOCK BOOK

First published in the UK 1997
by Ward Lock
Wellington House
125 Strand
London WC2R 0BB

A Cassell Imprint

A British Library Cataloguing in Publication Data block for
this book may be obtained from the British Library

ISBN 0 7063 7643 9

Designed by Yvonne Dedman

Printed and bound in Great Britain
by Mackays of Chatham

Contents

···

Be courageous. It's the only place left uncrowded.

Anita Roddick

Introduction

The Working Parent's Survival Guide has been written for working parents everywhere and for families of all shapes and sizes. It aims to inform, enlighten and inspire. Above all I hope that it empowers you to do much more than merely survive.

Parenthood is a terrific experience, most of the time! Being a working parent should not be allowed to cast a cloud over that experience – as seems to happen all too often these days – or interfere too much with enjoying life in general. With the right tools to hand it won't.

This guide sets out to give you those tools, or many of them at least. As with any set of instruments they are yours to do what you will with them. As long as they put you in control of the outcome they will have served their purpose.

A book you can dip into at any stage of parenting, first-time parents-to-be and parents of very young children will find The Working Parent's Survival Guide especially useful. It is probably at this stage, more than at any other time, that you have the opportunity to take stock of your working life and make those changes that you have up to now simply wondered about – perhaps retrain for a job that will give you more satisfaction and be altogether more compatible with family life. It also offers partners the opportunity to discuss the option of scaling back on work while the children are little ('downshifting' in today's parlance), and which one might do it – or perhaps consider the notion of both partners scaling back for a time. (Although it is also true that you can have a new lease of life and change direction when your children are grown up and independent.)

From both my professional knowledge and personal experience (mine and others), the book covers everything you need to know about being a working parent, from pregnancy to child care to relationships, to successfully reconciling your own needs as an individual with those of your job and family, to influencing your workplace, to knowing your statutory rights – but does not preach. The book is not aimed at encouraging parents to work but at enabling you to do so if you want to, and helping you adjust if you feel obliged to earn an income when you would rather be at home – all with the well-being of children to the fore.

Occasionally a spate of 'feminist backlash' type of media articles crop up, written by women who profess regret at 'putting their careers before their children', implying that doing so was a denial of their natural womanly role and thus harmful to their children. Such articles serve merely to strike fear and guilt into the heart of every loving parent; I have little patience with them. Even less so when they are sparked by the writer arriving at a personal crossroad – such as splitting from a partner, reaching 40 or simply a dead-end in their career. As someone who remained at home more or less full-time until my eldest child was 13, my relationship with my children is no better and no worse than a parent who made a different choice. Neither do I think my children necessarily benefited by having me around them so much. In fact I think I might have been a better person to live with had I been a 'working' mother with a job I enjoyed.

My own recollection of full-time mothering is of being constantly cross. We lived in cramped accommodation and were often short of money and I can tell you life for the children was far from idyllic. Oh yes, I baked and cooked

nutritious meals, took them to the park a lot, read and sang
to them at bedtime, but this rosy scene of motherhood hid
much impatience and frustration behind the scenes.
(Something that now causes me guilt and shame, although
my children, aged 25 and 20, seem to have fond memories
of their childhood.) While I adored my children I did not
enjoy being at home all day and longed for additional fulfilment in another role other than wife and mother. I longed
especially to be financially independent.

I'm inclined to think therefore that the human condition
means we are never happy with what we have and makes us
long for the greener grass on the other side. And that the
regrets that some parents feel at 'missing out on their children's childhood' have more to do with a rose-tinted view of
what they would like family life to be like than with reality.
(Incidentally, unless these parents were absent from home
every day I don't understand how they can have missed out
entirely on watching their children grow, or spending time
with them. What were they doing when they weren't at
work for goodness sake?)

To be a good and loving parent, you do not have to devote
yourself to your children 24 hours a day. As a working parent, it makes sense, however, to balance work and home
responsibilities: to make sure work doesn't encroach too
much on family time; to give yourself plenty of time to find
and choose child care and to be happy with your choice; to
be comfortable with whatever
decision you make about the
way you run your household; to
accept that from time to time
you will have to compromise,
both at work and at home; not
to feel a victim of circumstances beyond your control; to

*I find friends, allies and networks
very helpful. I have designed my
life around my need to work. Much
as I love my children, I find them
much more stressful than being at
work ...*

Accountant, mother of two

9

get your priorities right; and to have a pragmatic outlook on life and a good sense of humour.

These are all factors that help control the stresses of modern life and that by definition will mean you are better equipped to enjoy your dual roles. Ultimately, being surrounded by happy loving adults has more effect on a child's well-being than the number of actual hours spent with them.

... A child living in a family with a reasonable earned income, and modest but satisfactory housing, will have no more behaviour problems than one living in an affluent family, luxuriously housed.

Professor Phillip Graham, National Children's Bureau, House of Commons Health Committee, Fourth Report, Child and Adolescent Mental Health Services, March 1997

In this book I have sought to provide you with the means of controlling your own destiny, prompting you to be imaginative and creative, and to look to make as much use as possible of all opportunities to influence your workplace for the better. *The Working Parent's Survival Guide* deliberately focuses on your needs, a parent who also happens to work, rather than the specific needs of children, because, to paraphrase a more famous saying, support the parent and you nurture the child.

Note: The problem of whether to refer to your child as a boy or girl in this book is solved by sometimes using 'he' and sometimes 'she'. This is no more satisfactory than any other method, but it seemed to be the simplest approach.

CHAPTER 1

Pregnancy and its implications

Whether planned or otherwise, the moment pregnancy is confirmed all sorts of emotions are triggered. In a matter of seconds a parent-to-be can go from squealing with joy to panicking about how she or he will cope, wondering whether this was such a good idea after all. Happily for the preservation of the human race, once born most parents say that they wouldn't be without their children. Being a parent and holding down a job does, however, add an extra dimension to the whole experience. No longer 'retiring' to the home full-time when they start a family, millions of women, for a variety of reasons and in all corners of the world, now return to work soon after the birth of their babies. In the closing stages of the 1990s, families with both parents working is the norm rather than the exception.

Changes in community life have more or less put an end to automatic access to an extended network of family, friends and neighbours. With yesterday's traditions being out of step with modern society, a woman with a partner will naturally expect him to take equal responsibility for the children and the household. And most men concur with this expectation. However, research indicates that even the most equal of partnerships – both working, sharing domestic chores such as shopping, cooking, housework – comes to an abrupt end once the baby is born. Quite often the mother reverts and assumes all the responsibility for the house and children. At the same time, the father's career takes on greater significance, leaving him little time for domestic chores.

Greater involvement in domestic life helps men to put the stresses of work into perspective, and can remind them that they work to live, not live to work. Men may be surprised at how fulfilling family life can be.

Cary Cooper, Professor of Organisational Psychology, University of Manchester

Research has also found, however, that couples who have clear demarcation lines – one *always* doing the cooking, the other *always* doing the shopping, for example – fare better, managing to carry on as before after embarking on parenthood.

Start right

As it would appear then that the rules of joint working parenthood are best forged before the birth of the baby, the first survival tips are therefore aimed at couples about to become new parents – especially the female partner because it is she who will bear the brunt of any fall-out resulting from an unequal partnership. Focusing during the months of pregnancy on the issues that are bound to impact on your relationship and your working lives after the baby has been born gives you time to iron out any misunderstandings about assumptions and expectations, and to set strong foundations for the other stages of family life; this leaves you free to enjoy the baby when it comes. The following are some of the points that help to set this up:

I move heaven and earth to make sure nothing prevents me keeping my dinner date with my wife every Thursday night.

City stockbroker

• Attend antenatal clinics and parentcraft classes as a couple. Fathers who become involved in the lives of their children early on continue to do so as their children grow.

• Talk about your parenting expectations and aspirations, both of each other and for your children.

• Discuss what adjustments are likely to be needed to raise a child and accommodate the need to work. Talk about whether one of you will scale work down while the children are little, and the implications for that person's career. The opening section of Chapter 3, Back to Work?, will help you focus on the issues raised by a decision of this nature.

• Discuss how the household chores will be divided up, and agree a minimum level of standards. There is little point sharing the load if one of you ends up going over what the other has done because it didn't quite measure up. Talk about what annoys you most about your partner's house-keeping – for instance, the way it's done or the way it's allowed to pile up – and reach a compromise. Constant criticism will make the other person give up altogether.

• Air grievances as soon as they pop up. Never let resent-ments build up; eventually they can destroy relationships.

• Adopt as your motto the oft-repeated advice 'never go to bed or part without making up'; this will see you through many a trying time while you adjust to being parents.

Single and pregnant

Some women choose to become mothers without the sup-port of a partner, or split up with their partners during pregnancy. Life for the single working parent is not the same as that for two parents. It *can* be tougher, but it can also be easier in some ways. Two people in a relationship are constantly having to consider the feelings of the other, or to renegotiate the terms of their 'contract'. Many couples with two salaries remark on the hassle they get from each other. '*Oh, he'll help alright,*' she'll say, '*but boy do I have to plead to get him to!*' '*She's constantly nagging me,*' he'll say. '*If she left me alone I'd get round to it in my own time!*' Without wishing to seem flippant, at least the single parent knows where she stands and that she has to find extra strengths within herself. If you are a single parent, this book is for you too. All the advice about employment rights, child care, keeping your stress levels down, and balancing work and home applies equally to you as to families with two parents.

Contact the National Council for One Parent Families and Gingerbread (see Appendix IV) to make sure that you get all the benefits you are entitled to. For example, if you receive family credit or disability allowance, you may be able to have up to £60 a week of your income disregarded if you pay for child care. Worth up to £42 a week, this could rise to £57.30 a week if you are also getting Housing and Council Tax Benefit. Gingerbread can

Years of pleading with my partner to muck in and do his bit finally took its toll. I left him. I'd have done it sooner if I had known how wonderful it was going to be not to be constantly nagging and being able to make decisions without having to wait to consult him all the time.

Finance manager

If I think of the elements that impact on my ability to operate, then uppermost is the health and happiness of my three-year-old daughter. This depends most crucially on good quality child care, which, for as long as I am able to pay for it, is not too much of a problem.

Management consultant

also link you with a support group in your area. Contact with other single parents might provide you with invaluable support for yourself, and child care back-up for when you return to work.

My husband and partner of sixteen years, the one who wanted a baby for much longer than I had, the one who was deliriously happy when I announced I was pregnant, the one who was irretrievably 'in love' with someone else three months later, finally walked out on us when my daughter was three months old. My daughter is now 18 months old and a constant source of joy and pleasure. I have learned to cope with it all by looking at all the wonderful things I have instead of dwelling on all the things I don't.

Librarian

Pregnancy and the workplace

In the section Statutory Rights we look in detail at what you need to do at various stages of your pregnancy to make sure you maintain your statutory rights, and fulfil your legal obligations to your employer. It might be a good idea to read that section before telling your boss, or your colleagues, that you are pregnant. (Don't worry if you have already, there are no dire warnings in it: it simply alerts you to your legal rights.)

Trouble ahead?

Once you have told your boss, you may become aware of changes taking place in your relationship. Comments may be made about the department being disrupted while you are on maternity leave. Or you might find yourself being left off training schedules, excluded from forward planning

15

meetings or not being invited to apply for promotion. If you notice changes in behaviour towards you that bother you, challenge them tactfully. You might find it useful to point out that, because maternity leave is anticipated, contingency plans for cover while you are away can be made well in advance, unlike disruption caused by unplanned sickness absence. What's more, any company worth its salt should be interested in protecting its investments, of which you are one. Try dropping the odd statistic about the cost of training and recruitment, and the value of retaining experienced staff, within earshot of your boss. For example, GCHQ (part of the Civil Service) recently estimated that retaining four women scientists after maternity leave had saved it £93,100 – per person.

My boss was marvellous when I told him I was pregnant. A dad himself, he took as much interest in how everything was progressing as my partner. When I went back after the baby was born there was no problem about my going part-time.

Office secretary

However, if you are concerned that you really are being discriminated against – which can sometimes be very subtle and hard to label – make a note of incidents that bother you. Talk them over with your partner or a friend. It could be that your perception of the situation is letting you get things totally out of proportion. Maternity Alliance or the Equal

He made it clear he would not take kindly to my returning part-time.

Charity sector worker

My employer's reaction when I told him I was pregnant was 'bloody hell!'. It upset me dreadfully so I had to leave his office. When I went back in he apologised and asked what my plans were. I was on edge the whole time after that. I feared he would sack me if I put one foot wrong. I didn't go back there after the baby was born.

Storeroom clerk

Opportunities Commission will advise you professionally on whether or not you are being discriminated against – both are listed in Appendix IV. The notes you make will be particularly useful for this purpose.

How to tell colleagues

For most people letting colleagues know they are pregnant is a quiet affair, usually involving those with whom they work closely, who usually respond with warm congratulations. But some pregnant women worry about how the news will be received. You'll be able to gauge the reaction you are likely to have by the kind of environment you work in. If you are in any way anxious that your news won't be welcomed, maybe because your workplace isn't very pro working parents, making a proud and cheerful public announcement might help dissolve any negative rumblings. Putting a notice on the bulletin board, in the company newsletter or sending an e-mail message round the department is one way of doing this. If you felt like it you could turn your announcement into an invitation to celebrate your news with you, perhaps something like: 'Melissa Cook and Sean Dean are delighted to announce they are expecting a baby in June. Join us after work tonight in the Cat & Fiddle for a celebratory drink. Arrive after 7pm and you'll be too late.' Or whatever you feel is appropriate.

Inviting colleagues to share in the event will make it harder for them to be mean spirited later on, should they be so inclined. It can also help overcome any embarrassment colleagues might feel about acknowledging your pregnancy, for instance, if you are the only female in a male-dominated department. If you do take this route, be sure to tell your boss before going public! And invite him or her to any celebrations involving colleagues.

Atmospheric changes

By and large most women find that colleagues take their pregnancy in their stride. Others notice subtle changes that leave them feeling a bit sidelined, no longer 'one of the crowd'. Changes in relationships with colleagues may manifest themselves in a number of ways: those without children might stop inviting you to socialise with them outside work hours, for instance. Perhaps because they feel you will have nothing in common, or that you will bore them to death with baby talk. They may also fear the responsibility of looking after someone in the advance stages of pregnancy! Sometimes a climate of resentment is sparked off because non-parent colleagues perceive those with children as getting preferential treatment, perhaps because the company operates family friendly practices, which they feel they don't benefit from.

If you want to avoid problems with colleagues, the following points could help:

• Don't go on at length about your pregnancy; this will help non-parent colleagues quickly come to see that you are essentially the same person, as committed to your job as ever, but with a new talent to add to your skills.

Because I was ill a lot in the first three months of my pregnancy I was off work a fair bit. My work piled up and I sensed that my colleagues were feeling miffed with me. This taught me to plan ahead for unforeseen problems. Now I have become incredibly organised and have a plan of action about what happens to my work if I am off. Mainly it still waits for me to come back, but I now keep a list in my briefcase of everything in progress so that I can tell colleagues what to send me to work on at home. This means I am also able to warn my colleagues about any implications for them.

Local government officer

• Bring resentment out in to the open; this may stop mutterings of preferential treatment. If you feel brave enough, ask colleagues whether you have offended them. It may be that, when you are off for antenatal clinics and the like, a colleague is having to pick up some of your work. Alerting them in advance of when you are going to be off will reduce feelings of being 'dumped upon'. Whatever the reason, getting to the bottom of it will help you deal with it.

• Seek out the company of other colleagues with children for moral support.

Beating the clock

It has been said that a woman who goes through pregnancy with an air of calmness produces a calm and placid baby. True or not, being calm will certainly make you feel good, and is worth trying in the interests of having a baby who sleeps at night! Chapter 5, Dealing with Stress, looks at the subject more broadly. Here the focus is on pressure of work and how you might keep it to a manageable level. Caught up in the frenetic day-to-day struggle of keeping on top of heavy workloads, often resulting in a working week of 60 hours or more, it is all too easy to forget that it doesn't have to be like that.

Most people who work long hours in order to get the work done tend to blame the corporate culture. If this is the case with you there may indeed be little that you can do to change it – in the short term. But don't let that stop you trying. It is possible to influence your working environment for the better: Chapter 4, Alternative Ways of Working, offers many ideas and suggestions as to how you can go about tackling a working environment that is not family friendly – those who dare ....

Sometimes, however, working long hours can become a way of life. Look again at all those time management tips

I never felt better than when I was pregnant. I was so full of energy I worked even longer hours!

Solicitor

that people like me often trot out, and which most of us dismiss because we don't have the time to act on them! Nevertheless they do work. Most of them are just common sense, and from time to time we need reminding of them. If you can whittle back on excessive work hours now, not only will you feel a whole lot better for it, it will also help you to see if your job lends itself to a more permanent reduction in your hours after the baby is born – an option that you might want to consider. In case you can't find your list of time management mantras, there is one below:

• Do your background reading when you're travelling to and from work, if you can.

• Set a time limit on 'phone calls and meetings.

• Deal with routine jobs such as filing or returning 'phone calls in batches once a week. Be ruthless about throwing unwanted mail in the bin; if you can't read it now you certainly won't be able to read it in six months' time.

• Prioritise your workloads. Do the task you dread the most first! Then the rest in order of priority. Try never to leave a task unfinished.

I became more relaxed about the house and stopped trying to keep it in sparkling order. I went to bed early instead, which made a lot of difference to my energy levels the next day.

Local government officer

• Even if you are not the boss behave like one. Delegate as much as you can and learn to say no politely but effectively. (A good self-esteem/personal effectiveness session will help give you the skills for this.)

• Schedule a few hours into your time management programme each week just for you. Get away from your desk
for at least one hour each day, preferably out in the fresh air.
Never eat lunch at your desk.

While you are pregnant you might find this relatively easy to
do. After all, everyone expects a pregnant woman to take
care of her health. The challenge lies in continuing to find
some time for yourself once you are a working mother.
Getting into the habit now of taking time out to recharge
your batteries will stand you in good stead later.

Men and pregnancy

After the obligatory congratulations, fathers-to-be tend to
be relegated to the chorus line as regards preparation for
parenthood. The world at large assumes you are thrilled at
the prospect, and then turns the spotlight back onto your
partner. If you are about to become a father for the first time
this chapter gives you an opportunity to explore your emotions, reactions and expectations of parenthood – either
aloud to your partner or a friend, or in your head if you prefer. If you are a father already, it gives you a chance to think
back and maybe resolve some old issues still lying around. It
also offers you some suggestions about how not to let work
get in the way of getting to know, and spending time with,
your child.

Responsible feelings

Your response to the news that your partner is pregnant is
likely to be similar to hers, although you may not feel quite
so comfortable about expressing your thoughts openly. Men

who are already fathers recall experiencing a range of emotion: excitement at the prospect of a baby to carry on the family line, hearts bursting with renewed love for their partners, depression at the loss of what they perceive to be the end of their carefree days, and fear ... at the sheer responsibility of it all and the financial implications of bringing up a child, which are not insignificant. (Surveys pitch this at anything between £4,300 and £18,867 in the first three years of life alone!) The months of pregnancy can be a worrying time for the new dad-to-be. And talking to other first time dads-to-be may not help either. Few it seems are prepared to come clean and say how they really feel – perhaps because they don't have anything to compare their feelings with as yet and are not sure how they are supposed to feel.

I still work extremely hard and I'm seldom home before my kids are in bed, but no matter what is going on at work the weekend is family time.

City banker

Friends who are already fathers are much more likely to tell you how they felt about imminent fatherhood, their fears and joys on becoming a father, and pass on tips they wished they had been given. They will also tell you that your heart will melt when your baby looks at you for the first time, and how the experience of becoming a parent is like no other. Nevertheless, making friends with new dads-to-be can provide you with a source of support in the months leading up to the birth of the baby, and mates with something in common afterwards. Going to antenatal classes with your partner gives you an opportunity to meet other like-minded people.

Having my daughter fall asleep in my arms gives me a feeling I can't describe.

Construction worker

Share whatever you are feeling with your partner. She'll be feeling just as happy, just as insecure and just as fearful about the future as you are. You'll have a lot in common! If you want to talk to a professional about your feelings contact Exploring Parenthood or The Parent Network. Both run helplines and a network of local parent's support groups. You'll find them listed at the back.

Preparation for fatherhood

Although you may have difficulty getting time off to attend antenatal clinics and parenting classes with your partner, fathers who have managed this say that it made all the difference to how they felt in the delivery room and in the first few months of their child's life. Even if you have to lie about why you want the time off, following the various stages of pregnancy first hand, and getting used to being around the medics, will help you feel less 'in the way' when your partner goes into labour. Giving birth is a new experience for first-time mothers too, and can be scary. Having two of you asking questions of the professionals will prepare you better for when the baby is born. (Incidentally, there is some evidence to suggest that home delivery births help fathers feel more involved during the birth of their child and aid bonding. Although not an option for everyone it is worth discussing it with your partner and the medical professionals taking care of her.)

I felt in the way, and cross with myself for not asking more questions about the 'mechanics' of labour.

New dad

When it was all over the midwife left, I changed the bed while Wendy had a shower then we all cuddled up together in our own bed and slept. It was a wonderful feeling.

New dad, second family

Changes in your partner

Beside the very obvious one of changes to the shape of her body your partner's emotions during pregnancy and in the first year of your baby's life could be somewhat unpredictable. One minute she may be wonderfully happy and unable to do enough for you, the next minute she could be packing her bag and walking out the door – or telling you to go. If you are left reeling and bewildered by the changes in your partner – and each woman experiences pregnancy and motherhood in her own way, so how your friend's partner is or was during her pregnancy is no guarantee that your partner is going to be the same – tell her so! Together you can find a way for you to live through these moments emotionally intact. Having a sense of humour about it is probably the best therapy of all. Take care not to belittle your partner's mood swings by laughing at her though. Then you'll really be in trouble!

Just good friends

Having been the centre of each other's universe, it can be hard to adjust to the changes a baby imposes on a relationship, even before it makes its appearance. For one thing, if your partner feels nauseous much of the time it's hard for her to feel amorous. But even if, in the early stages at least, your partner's pregnancy doesn't interrupt your sex life you are bound to experience some changes in the emotional content of your relationship. It's inevitable. The developing baby will take up more and more of your partner's attention. You might catch her lovingly stroking or holding her belly with an expression on her face that she once reserved for you, and you may very well feel a spot of jealousy. Or you could be in the middle of a romantic cuddle, and just as you are both beginning to feel a rush of anticipation … the baby gives a hearty kick! Your partner's attention is instantly riveted on the goings on in her body, the baby's not yours … you may be left high and dry, so to speak. If you had someone playing football with your insides you too would find it hard to concentrate on sex! Laugh about it. After all, you don't have to have full intercourse to be intimate and sexual, there are other ways of giving each other pleasure. Talk about this aspect of your relationship more. It'll be good preparation for after the birth, when most couples experience a cooling of ardour for a little while, primarily brought on by lack of sleep and sheer exhaustion.

Career versus family life

In common with women, the arrival of a baby is often the catalyst for men to take stock of long-term career and job prospects. Unlike women, however, who tend to downshift while the children are young, the birth of a child prompts most men to work harder. For 'harder' in this case read 'long working hours', the main cause of blight on family life in the 1990s. The longer the hours worked the less opportunities fathers have to take part in family activities, and the more likely it is that mothers assume sole responsibility for the children. The point of embarkation to fatherhood is a good time to consider the impact of work on the ability to spend time on family life.

The workplace has never been more favourably disposed than now towards employees who want to lead balanced lives. With the cost to industry of stress-related illness – primarily resulting from overwork (British men work the longest hours in Europe) – estimated to cost the UK economy between £7 billion and £12 billion a year, more and more companies are recognising that people with lives outside of work are more effective and productive in the workplace. Chapters 4 and 5 look at ways in which individuals can achieve this for themselves.

For advice on how to influence your organisation's corporate culture contact the following organisations (see Appendix IV for addresses):

• Employers For Childcare
• Parents At Work
• The Industrial Society
• Trades Union Congress (TUC)
• Opportunity 2000
• Equal Opportunities Commission.

They can provide you with the business case for change, something most employers respond to, or they may be able to set the ball rolling within your company themselves – without reference to you. See also the examples of the business benefits of family-friendly practices in Chapter 4, Alternative Ways of Working.

Take advice too from an organisation called Campaign Against Bullying At Work (CABAW). This was launched at the House of Lords in January 1996 by a man who had been bullied out of his job – caused by pressure of work and long hours which his employer failed to acknowledge – and into a nervous breakdown.

It is very clear that men's attitudes to parenting and work are changing fast, and for many reasons. They want to retain their career but they also want to break free of the stereotypical role that causes them to miss so much of their children's development. Too many older men feel they missed the boat because they didn't invest during the early years, ending up feeling estranged from their children as they got older.

Psychologist

In addition, sound out the views of your colleagues about working practices that are family and employee friendly to gauge whether there is potential for setting up a workplace support group. A group of people is always a more effective force for change than a lone voice.

Taking paternity leave

Currently, the UK does not grant fathers a statutory right to paternity leave. And while, in practice, quite a number of UK companies allow fathers-to-be from two to ten days of paternity leave on the birth of a child, it tends to be unpaid, forcing some men to have to choose between being present at the birth of their child and keeping the family coffers healthy. If it is at all possible, take time off when your baby is born. Those first few days after birth are quite magical, and can't be recovered. A number of UK organisations are

....

When our second child was due I decided to approach my employer about taking some time off from work. I had no idea how my request would be received. 'What on earth do you want to do that for?' 'This will damage your career prospects' were among some of the reactions I expected. To my surprise I received a very sympathetic hearing. The business case I put to my employers was quite simply that a healthy domestic environment is an important and necessary basis for ensuring continued good performance at work ...

Those who doubt the validity of this should think about how often they have seen a personal difficulty adversely affect colleagues at work. I took an initial five week break followed by three months of working two and a half days a week. After that it was business as usual.

Senior management consultant

actively campaigning for fathers to have a statutory right to paternity leave. As I write we have just had a General Election and the new (Labour) government is reviewing its position with regard

When my daughter was born I was lucky enough to be able to take six weeks off so I could get to know her at this lovely stage and to have a period of solid time together as a family.

Surveyor

to opting in to the EU Social Chapter. If this goes ahead we are likely to see a Parental Leave Directive implemented in June 1998. Apart from more general employment rights, the effect would amount to UK working parents at last having a statutory right to paternity leave. Check the current position with Employers for Childcare, Parents At Work, Trades Union Congress (TUC) or Maternity Alliance (for addresses see Appendix IV).

Statutory rights

Accurate at the time of writing, changes in employment legislation do occur from time to time, so use the following as a guide to your minimum rights. For an update on the current position, or for more detailed advice with regard to your own particular situation, contact Maternity Alliance, your local Citizens Advice Bureau, the Rights of Women or the Equal Opportunities Commission (see Appendix IV).

If you are going abroad to another European Union country contact Citizens First on 0800 581591 for free information booklets about employment rights, and on the education system for school-age children, in the country to which you are relocating. Anyone relocating to a country outside the EU should be able to get this type of information from that country's UK Embassy, High Commission or other elected representative before going – though you may need to ask weeks, if not months, ahead. If your company is relocating you, ask the personnel department to do the research on your behalf. Readers in other countries need to check out their rights locally. (See Appendix III for examples of other countries' statutory parental rights.)

Antenatal leave

All pregnant employees in the UK are entitled to paid time off for antenatal care, including attending relaxation and parent craft classes. Your employer may want to see a certificate confirming your pregnancy, from a registered medical practitioner, midwife or health visitor as well as proof that an appointment has been made – which you can provide only once you have had your first check-up, of course. Some employers mistakenly think this is time off at your own expense, and some have attempted to dismiss employees who insist otherwise. If you have an experience of this nature, contact Maternity Alliance for advice on what to do if your employer denies you this right.

Maternity leave

Currently, all working mothers in the UK have the right to fourteen weeks of maternity *leave*, regardless of how many hours you work or how long you have worked for your present employer. People who have been with the same employer for two years by the time they are eleven weeks away from giving birth are entitled to an additional period of maternity *absence* of twenty-six weeks, making a total of forty weeks in all. These rights may also apply to mothers who give birth to a stillborn baby at or after twenty-four weeks' gestation.

Right to return

At least twenty-one days before you intend to begin your maternity leave, tell your employer formally in writing that you are pregnant and the date the baby is due, usually confirmed with a medical certificate. If you are able to take advantage of the full forty weeks' leave of absence, then state at the same time your intention to return to your job. You also need to give the date you want your maternity leave and Statutory Maternity Pay (SMP) to start from. Generally speaking maternity leave starts on the date you stop working whereas SMP starts from the Sunday after that date – and can't be paid earlier than eleven weeks before your baby is due.

If you are only entitled to the statutory fourteen weeks' leave you don't have to tell your employer the date of your return, although it might be diplomatic to do so. In your case you have an automatic right to return to your job, with the same terms and conditions – as long as you return at the end of the fourteen weeks.

When my employer wrote to me while I was on maternity leave to ask me to confirm that I was returning to work, I truly didn't realise that if I didn't reply in writing I risked losing my job. As I was ill at the end of my maternity leave I sent a letter to my employer explaining I couldn't return just yet, enclosing a medical certificate. Imagine my shock when I got a letter back saying that my contract had been terminated because I hadn't confirmed in writing that I was planning to return. I thought that as I had told my employer I would be returning when I went on leave this would be enough. With legal help I took my case to an Industrial Tribunal which found in my favour. However, the compensation I won didn't make up for the loss of my job.

Hotel worker

Women taking extended leave also have this right, unless: your original job is no longer available, perhaps for redundancy reasons, or it isn't reasonably practical for you to be given back your original job, which can apply particularly in the case of employers of five or fewer people. If this happens to you, don't accept your employer's decision without question. Check the facts of your case with an independent organisation such as Rights of Women, Maternity Alliance or a Citizen's Advice Bureau.

It's important that you give your employer all the required notifications within the right time limits, otherwise you could lose some of your statutory maternity rights. You now have a number of workplace rights to protect you and your baby during your pregnancy, including not being made redundant simply because you are pregnant. Not all employers know or understand the law. Make sure you do. If you have any doubts contact Maternity Alliance.

Adoption leave

As yet parents in the UK have no legal right to adoption leave and pay. In practice, however, many employers grant employees leave to attend meetings before adopting, as well as a period of leave once adoption is completed. Though a recent survey of 243 British companies, conducted by the Industrial Relations Services, found the average amount of time off was thirty-two weeks, this ranged from just two days to sixty-three weeks – the younger the child being adopted the longer the leave allowed. Seventy-three per cent of the respondents to the survey paid a part of the time allowed off, ranging from six weeks on full pay and twenty-four weeks on half-pay to two weeks on full pay for a child under five. There is obviously great inconsistency concerning adoption leave and pay. At the time of writing, there are moves afoot to introduce legislation to extend statutory maternity leave and pay to adoptive parents. Check the current position with Maternity Alliance.

Health and safety at work

If the type of work you do could endanger your health and that of your unborn baby, your employer is required by law to take steps to prevent this happening – perhaps by moving you to other suitable alternative work. If this isn't possible, then your employer may be required to suspend you, on full pay, until you are able to resume your job.

Maternity pay

Statutory Maternity Pay is commonly referred to as SMP. If you earn enough to pay National Insurance Contributions (NICs) and you have been with the same employer for at least twenty-six weeks with fifteen weeks to go before the birth of your baby, you qualify for up to eighteen weeks of pay. Normally, the first six weeks is paid at ninety per cent of your average salary in the preceding eight weeks, with the remaining twelve paid at the statutory lower rate, which changes annually. In the tax year 1997–98 this was set at £55.70 per week. Some employers offer better terms than the statutory minimum, in a number of cases paying as much as full salary for six months. Check your contract to see what terms and conditions your employer offers. Ask for information from your personnel department too, if you have one, because you may not be in possession of recent changes to your company's employment policies.

SMP is not paid as well as your salary. If you return to work at the end of fourteen weeks, you lose the remaining four weeks of SMP.

Through your National Insurance Contributions you have paid towards your Statutory Maternity Pay and Maternity Allowance, so you do not pay this money back to your employer should you decide not to return to the same job. Check what your contract says if you benefit from better than statutory terms. For instance, some employers require employees to return to work for a certain period of time in order to qualify for enhanced pay and leave.

If you are self-employed, recently unemployed or you have changed your job since becoming pregnant, you probably won't get SMP, but you will be able to claim Maternity Allowance as long as you paid at least twenty-six NICs in the sixty-six weeks leading up to the birth of your baby. But don't get too excited. Self-employed and unemployed women currently get £48.35 a week, while those who changed their jobs get £55.70 a week – for a maximum of eighteen weeks in each case.

If you are off with a pregnancy-related illness in the six weeks before your baby is born, you may find your maternity leave period automatically triggered from the first day that you are ill. A pregnancy-related illness before this time should be treated on the same terms as any other illness, that is, it should not be counted as maternity leave and paid as sick leave. Seek advice if your employer views it otherwise.

Parental leave

Currently, most European Union countries grant this form of leave to employees as a statutory right; the UK, however, does not. By the end of 1998 at the latest, employees in all EU countries, with the exception of the UK, will be able to claim this leave. Granted under the Parental Leave Directive, campaigning organisations are lobbying for the same right to be extended to employees in the UK, which would allow parents a minimum of three months' parental leave – to be taken at any time between birth and a child's eighth birthday. Check out the current position with Maternity Alliance.

Family leave

Most EU countries also grant employees a statutory right to an annual number of days' leave for family reasons – illness, accidents and emergencies, domestic problems, deaths, marriages and the like. In most cases the leave is paid, ranging from up to four days on full pay (France) to sixty days a year to care for sick relatives on seventy-five per cent of salary (Sweden). Though not a statutory right in the UK, in practice many British companies also allow a number of days off a year for family reasons. Check the current statutory position with a specialist organisation – such as the Department for Employment, Trades Union Congress (TUC) or the Work and Family Unit of the Equal Opportunities Commission (see Appendix IV). (Parental leave and family leave are rights granted to employees under the EU Social Chapter. As I write we have just had a General Election. The new government is taking a different view on adopting these rights, so check the current position with Maternity Alliance.)

Contractual terms

Just to confuse everyone, by law your contractual terms and conditions continue for the period of statutory maternity *leave* (which amounts to fourteen weeks), but not necessarily for the period of extended *absence* – unless of course your contract states otherwise. For example, during this period annual holidays continue to accrue as normal, your employer should continue to pay towards any existing pension plan, you keep the use of your company car, you are entitled to pay increments, etc. In short, apart from paying your salary, your employer treats you exactly the same as if you were still at work.

How women who are entitled to leave *and* absence fare is not so clear cut. In theory you are still under contract during leave of absence so you might expect your terms and conditions to apply during the whole of your time off work. In practice, however, it would seem that your contract becomes frozen at the end of the maternity leave period, resuming again when you return to work. With no automatic right to protection of benefits after your fourteen weeks of maternity leave are up, you may have to negotiate on this point with your employer. Check out the finer details of your own situation, as well as where you stand with regard to accumulated annual leave, statutory holidays and pay rises while on extended maternity absence, with a specialist organisation, such as Maternity Alliance (see Appendix IV).

Exception to the rule?

Although it may be self-evident that not all the above apply to the self-employed and unemployed, it is perhaps less obvious that they may not always apply to members of the police force, masters or crew members engaged in share fishing (you could be pregnant in such circumstances, you know), and employees who normally work outside Great Britain under the terms of their contract – although most employees on offshore and gas installations in British sectors will be covered. Women who work for more than one employer will have separate maternity rights in relation to each. If you fall into one of these categories or if, for any other reason, you are unsure of where you stand, contact Maternity Alliance for advice (see Appendix IV).

CHAPTER 2

Parenthood

··

Adjusting to motherhood

In the advanced stages of pregnancy, many women long to
start their maternity leave, no doubt with one eye on the lux-
ury of not having to rise early and join the rugby scrum to
get to work. It can come as a surprise then to find feelings of
boredom and isolation setting in once the novelty of being at
home all day wears off. First-time mothers and mothers who
have as yet made no friends where they live can be especially
prone to feeling this way. Added to which can be the discov-
ery that motherhood isn't as easy as it's cracked up to be.
Some women seem to be born naturals, whereas others have
to work at it – not every woman is made for motherhood
temperamentally. If you find early feelings of euphoria and
delight in your baby giving way to exhaustion, anger, fear or
inadequacy, don't imagine that there is something wrong
with you. Talk about how you are feeling to your partner if
you have one, a friend if you haven't or seek some professional support if you feel you need it. You are not the first
parent to feel a bit shell-shocked after the birth of a baby,
and you won't be the last. Try not to let it worry you.

Helping hand

A new concept of help, an import from the USA, is a doula
(pronounced doo-la). A cross between a cook, cleaner,

mother's help and friend, a doula will shop, cook, tidy up and prop you up in those first few weeks after the baby's birth, all for around £30 for three hours. Trained to fill the gap left by no longer having mothers, sisters, grandmothers, friends and neighbours in attendance in the weeks after childbirth, a doula (which is the ancient Greek word for handmaiden) can be particularly useful for the second-time-around mother: looking after the baby when you need to spend time with your older child or vice versa. Although not as yet widespread throughout Britain, the importer of this new breed of parental support has plans to franchise it around the UK. For information on doulas in your area contact SupaCare on 0171 486 1997.

Some babies just seem to arrive in the world determined to make their parents feel bad, and they will succeed if you let them! The Parent Network, Exploring Parenthood and Meet-A-Mum Association are all organisations that can help

· ·

I was totally unprepared for motherhood. I just didn't think about it. I loved being pregnant and felt wonderfully well all the way through. Suddenly, here was this tiny person totally dependent on me. The intensity of emotions I felt terrified me. I swam between loving him fiercely to hating him for not letting me stop him crying. I didn't realise it but I was suffering from postnatal depression. With no friends or family near by there was no-one to talk to. It never occurred to me to see my doctor.

Thank goodness Susanna appeared. She stopped me one day as I was out shopping when my son was three months old, saying did I know we lived opposite each other (I didn't). She too had a small child – eight months older than mine – and would I like to have afternoon tea with her? I am eternally grateful to her. She rescued me from isolation, and my son from being battered!

Freelance journalist, single parent

you build confidence in yourself as a parent and prevent isolation taking hold. If you have a baby who cries a great deal and can't – or won't – be comforted, get advice from your GP, Health Visitor or baby clinic. In addition contact Cry-Sis, which offers a helpline between the hours of 8am and 11pm to provide support for parents with children who cry incessantly – a safety-valve for parents at breaking point. All these organisations are listed in Appendix IV.

It was the constant attention that got to me. This baby seemed to want me 24 hours a day. I had to sleep when she slept otherwise I would never have got any. When my husband came home I poured all my feelings of resentment and isolation out on him. He didn't understand. He kept asking why I wasn't stripping the walls.

Hospital administrator

Trust yourself

As a new mother you may be inundated with advice from seasoned mothers, your mother or mother-in-law. Don't reject it out of hand, feel threatened by it or feel they think you must be incapable of looking after your own child. It is likely to have more to do with a genuine wish to share their experiences with you and give you the benefit of learning from their mistakes. At the same time trust your own instincts. If you have an uneasy feeling about an aspect of child-rearing advice, don't ignore it. You know your child better than anyone else, you know how you want to raise him. You know when he is distressed about something. If you try to raise him by someone else's methods with which you are not entirely in tune, your child will pick up on your insecurity and be unsettled. The trick is to listen to and learn from the advice on offer, and adapt it to suit your own style of parenting.

Comrades in arms

If you formed friendships at antenatal classes, consolidate them now that you are on leave. Organise a coffee morning or arrange to meet in the park if there's one near you. Conversations with other new mothers can be a great source of comfort. You'll quickly learn that you are not the only one suffering from sleepless nights, tetchy relationships, jealous siblings, sore breasts, baby nappy rash, doubts about returning to work, etc. And if you do come across the mother with the inevitable angelic baby, console yourself that your baby probably has more fighting spirit!

Talking to other mothers is also a great way of letting off steam about your partner, a safety-valve that will help you get rid of pent-up frustrations and enable you to resolve any conflicts with a partner in a positive way. Time in their company also gives you permission to talk at length about your baby, because this is what they will be doing too. That way you won't have to experience the indignity of watching other friends' eyes glaze over as you tell them for the umpteenth time how adorable your baby is.

Neighbourhood watch

Building support networks where they live should be an objective of every working parent, especially a working mother, as soon as pregnancy announces itself. This advice is passed on from countless working parents who wish *they* had done it – not only for the support of like-minded people near by to call on for a chat or in an emergency, but also to help you survive in a child care crisis – as you will see when you get to Chapter 6. Your neighbours are the obvious place to start. Do a bit of watching from the windows to get an idea of the sort of people your neighbours are, if you don't know them already. You can learn a lot about them this way: their approximate ages, lifestyles, whether they have children. I'm advocating this with the purest of intentions, and merely as a convenient way of spotting like-minded people with whom to make friends.

Social watering holes

If among your neighbours you see someone you would like to get to know a bit more, but aren't sure about inviting them to your home just yet, strike up an acquaintance when you bump into each other at the local baker, greengrocer, in the queue at your local supermarket or simply when you pass in the street. You could say you are neighbours, you are taking a break from work, you are trying to get to know people living around you better – would she or he like to meet for coffee one morning? Other places to go include:

• Local church (or other religious meeting places), village or community centre fêtes.

• Open days at play groups, schools, mother and baby clubs.

• Visiting the children's library.

• Your favoured political party branch meetings.

Just being able to waste time wandering round the village and the shops has been great. I've become very friendly with my neighbours. I didn't have the time before.

District nurse

• Evening classes at your local college of further education.

Local support groups

Notice boards in libraries or listings in your local paper are other good sources of local contact points. Look out particularly for notices of meetings of local support groups for working parents, which are quite common these days. Alternatively, contact the National Childbirth Trust or Parents At Work which may be able to put you in touch with ones they know of locally. One introduction will lead to another, and without you even noticing it happening you will have acquired a wide circle of friends able to offer support for each other and provide ready-made playmates for the children.

When everything works, I feel I can control the events in my life as well as I could before I became a parent. At other times, I feel as though I am operating with my hands tied behind my back. Thank goodness for support networks.

Self-employed parent

House rules

Traditional husband and wife roles often come to the fore again after the birth of a baby, shown to be the case especially with couples who *share* the breadwinning and housework. Women often scale back on work to make room for a growing family at this point, leaving men's jobs to assume greater importance, possibly for financial or promotion reasons. In these circumstances the mother will often end up doing the bulk of the housework and care of the children. For some households this is not an issue, in others it is. Tension can be avoided by drawing up a 'division of labour' plan and agreeing how it will be shared out. Comparing notes once a month about how it's working out in practice is an opportunity to air grumbles before they become resentments, fine tuning as you go.

Sam picks Jenny up in the evenings, changes her, feeds her and has her ready for bed by the time I come home. Once we've settled her I cook us a meal.

Doctor

41

Allowing your partner time to adjust

Whereas most new mothers fall in love with their babies at
birth (though not always), fathers tend to come to the boil
more slowly – although being involved with their children
from birth may help them to bond quicker. However, some
men just cannot cope with small babies, often coming into
their own once the baby becomes a child. Sometimes men
who feel like this are frightened by the fragility of a new
baby. If your partner can't be persuaded to become involved
in the day-to-day routine of looking after his new baby,
accept this state of affairs for a while – and simply delegate
more of the household routine to him by way of compensa-
ting you for being on constant baby duty.

Asking for help

With a new baby household chores in general may get
thrown out of kilter for a while. You'll benefit from having a
relaxed attitude to this aspect of family life. Or, to give you
both a break, draw up a list of household chores and use it
to share out between all those friends and relations who ask
what they can do to help in the first few weeks after the
baby's birth – and who may never actually get round to
doing anything unless you take up their offers. People usually do mean it when they ask if there is something they can
do to help, but often prefer to be set a specific task rather
than leaving it up to them.

So, how about some pre-cooked meals for the freezer?
Doing the weekly shop, tending the garden, taking older
children off your hands for a bit, vacuum cleaning, ironing,
or coming round in the evening to help cope with a fractious baby. At a time when both you and your partner may
be feeling worn out, an experienced parent around to take a

turn pacing the floor, or to let you sit down to a meal secure in the knowledge that someone else will see to the baby for a bit, can bring much needed respite. You can repay the favours later on by throwing a party to thank everyone for their support.

Stoking the fires of desire

Wrapped up in a new baby, it's all too easy to let time with partners slide. Sex is often the first casualty of birth; lack of sleep sees to that. Exhausted already you may feel it's the last thing you want to do just now, seeing it as yet another demand on your time and feelings. You may long for your partner simply to give you a cuddle, while he may be under the impression that to make love to you reassures you that his feelings haven't changed. A meal alone together on a regular basis (you don't have to go out to do this) can be wonderful for nurturing relationships. Or try to make a point of sitting together each evening after the baby or children are in bed to catch up on each other's day. Or watch a video together. Couples who separate often speak of how they simply 'grew apart'. Spending time together as companions feeds relationships.

Making wild passionate love any time and all over the house got put on the back burner when Caroline was born. Now that she is going to bed earlier in the evenings we're starting to spend cuddly times together again.

Market trader

Older children

The arrival of a new brother or sister is a time when the needs of older children can get pushed aside. It's natural for parents to concentrate on the needs of the baby and leave older children to amuse themselves – sometimes out of sheer exhaustion. No matter what age the child, your relationship with her has to be fostered and fed, in much the same way as that with your partner or other adults in your life need to be kept alive. As children grow older and move on to secondary school it becomes particularly important and increasingly difficult to keep in touch with their lives. At this age parents tend to stop collecting them from school, often losing touch with who their friends are and the parents of their friends. This can be particularly costly when your child wants to stay overnight at a friend's house. What are the friend's parents like? Do they have the same attitude to parenting that you have? Will they leave your child and her friend alone in the house? Will they allow the children to watch an unsuitable video? By the time they are teenagers, you have absolutely no control over whom they see and what they get up to when you are not around – though they will still continue to impact on your life.

New parents will be able to set a precedent for spending time together with their children at all stages by lying down with a toddler to listen to a story tape while the baby is

When I took maternity leave for the second time I kept on my first child's carer. Though this cost a fair bit it turned out to have all sorts of pluses. I had more time to myself before the baby arrived and more time with the baby when she was born. The arrangement also worked the other way. I was able to leave the baby with the childminder and spend time with my older son. As I planned to return to work it meant that the new baby was used to her carer from birth. Although I didn't need to in the end, I had also arranged with my childminder that she would look after my son while I was giving birth.

Bank manager

feeding or, better still, asleep. This kills two birds with one stone: it gives you the chance to catch up on rest and your older child the feeling of special time with her. This might not work if you have more than one older child of course, in which case try watching a video together. If you find it impossible not to have the baby with you all the time, then fit the baby's routine around your older child's; it will be less wearing on you this way – unless of course your older child happens to be a teenager.

Good to talk

The occasional 'phone call or short note to friends, preferably about something you have in common rather than about the baby, will help keep these relationships ticking over until such time as you are able to get out again, or have the energy to invite them round. You could also suggest that they come round and entertain you. As your child gets older you will be glad that you cultivated these relationships and didn't lose touch with the world beyond babies.

Preparing your child for separation

Whether you return to work or not there will still be times when you will want to leave your child with someone else, be it a friend or a relative. Get your baby used to the idea of other people caring for her as early as possible. From birth make sure that your partner plays as active a role in her daily routine as you do. Leave them alone on a regular basis – even if only to lie down for an hour, go next door to a neighbour or down the street to the shops. Let friends and relatives play with her, change her, feed her, mind her. Children need to socialise widely and learn to interact with a range of people to help them get a more rounded view of the world. Nevertheless, leaving your child with someone else for the first time is yet another adjustment for new mothers to have to make.

Be kind to yourself when the time comes. Acknowledge it if you are upset and line up treats to take your mind off whether she is missing you – she probably won't be, at least not half as much as you are missing her! By the way, most six- to eight-month-old babies get anxious in the presence of strangers. It is simply a positive reaction to healthy bonding with their parents, certainly nothing to be anxious about.

Children who are the centre of their mother's universe feel stifled and over-responsible for her fulfilment.

Clinical psychologist

In touch with work

It's surprising how easy it is to lose touch with work when on leave. This is great for short periods of time such as annual leave, which allows you to unwind and shake off the stresses of office politics. However, to lose touch entirely over a long period of time can make your return more stressful than it need be. To find that while you have been away the office arrangement changed, new colleagues replaced old and the company took a different direction can be very traumatic, particularly because, as an old hand, you will be expected to pick up where you left off. No allowances will

My company operates a very good 'keeping in touch' system for people on leave. I got copies of bulletins and briefings and was invited to attend training and departmental meetings at the expense of the company. It made returning to work much easier than I thought it would be.

Civil Servant

be made for you as they might be for a new girl in class. To reduce the risk of this happening make preparations for keeping in touch with the goings on at work, both socially and professionally. Here are some ideas:

• Put yourself on mailing lists for company magazines or newsletters. Make sure that department memos, minutes of meetings, notices of training opportunities and social outings all come your way too.

• If your company does not have a system for dealing with eventualities like this, get a colleague to undertake to do it. Or, if you are being replaced temporarily while on leave, call up your replacement and ask her or him to send you copies of anything relevant to your work.

• Keep in fairly regular contact with your boss and people you work with. Call them once a month. Your return to work will be more smooth, you won't have lost touch with colleagues' professional development while you've been away, and you'll have reduced the chances of being left behind, or sidelined, while you were off busy being a parent.

I feel very apprehensive about going back. I'm afraid I'll be rusty or that I won't be put back with the same crowd.

Telephonist

Time for yourself

The work ethic being what it is it's a deliciously naughty feeling to literally put your feet up, give in to the wishes of family and friends to do things for you, and not have a sense of guilt about it! While having a baby is not an illness, you are likely to be tired, at least in the early months, and particularly if you worked right up to the birth. Rest whenever

*I'm great at organising the family,
I just can't seem to do the same
for myself.*

Driving instructor

you can, even if you have to do this at the same time as the baby sleeps, and go for walks in the fresh air. Your local community centre may run relaxation or yoga classes for new mothers, in which case they will also operate a crèche where you can leave your baby in safety while you have half an hour to yourself – this in itself can be relaxing.

Adjusting to fatherhood

The big moment arrives, your baby is about to be born. Emotions are high and all attention is focused on your partner. There you are in the delivery room, encouraging your partner to pant ... while she is possibly telling you to shut up and leave her alone! Or maybe you are hanging about in the father's room, feeling you'd be no help in the delivery room, and in any

I chickened out of being there at the birth at the last minute and I was very disappointed with myself afterwards. I was just glad it was all over and they were both well.

Gardener

case you would prefer not to know about the gory details, thank you very much. What do you feel? Panic? Trapped? Thrilled? Just how prepared for parenthood are you? And now here you are holding your new baby for the first time. Nothing quite prepares you for the emotion of that moment.

I cried all the way home from the hospital. It felt like the saddest day of my life. The happiest was when my son made his first 'real' sound at three months, and I was holding him in my arms.

Barrister

Mixed emotions

Once the dust has settled you may find yourself with all sorts of mixed emotions. Overwhelming love for your new baby, and a touch jealous of the attention he is getting from your partner. The longed-for return to 'normality' now that the baby is here doesn't happen. Almost all your partner's time and energy are taken up with the demands of the baby, as well as with her own need to preserve her strength, especially if she is going to return to work. You may be surprised to find yourself feeling uneasy about the way he seems to be permanently clamped to her breast. You may be irritated by having your meals and cosy times together constantly interrupted by the baby. You may feel rejected by him if you seem never to be able to stop him crying. Some new fathers even feel depressed. Although many men settle easily into the role of fatherhood, others take some time to adjust to it, rising to the challenge best when children are at the rough and tumble stage. Sometimes bonding with a baby is a matter of confidence. Holding him, changing him, bathing him and feeding him will all help to build your confidence in being able to take care of him, and help you to understand his needs more.

Jim wasn't a planned baby and I still hadn't accepted it when all of sudden he was here. To be honest I hadn't thought about what life would be like when he was born, I hadn't wanted to, I wasn't ready to be a father really. I had no great urge to pick him up and show him off and was more than happy to hand him over to Jenna when he cried. I don't think I resented him at first, but I was conscious of how much things had changed since he'd arrived. I'm much closer to him now that he can sit up and take notice of what's going on around him.

Local authority councillor

49

Whatever your feelings see them for what they are, the normal feelings of a new father who needs time to get used to the idea, and adjust to having a different relationship with his child's mother. Talk to your partner about how you are feeling. She may welcome being able to say that she too is struggling to adjust to parenthood. Contrary to what you might have been led to believe, falling in love with a baby, and knowing how to take care of it, doesn't necessarily come naturally to women either. You are in this together. Your capacity for caring and forming an attachment with your baby is equal. As also is your capacity to suffer from postnatal depression!

Not being able to eat without interruption, broken sleep and my wife's body belonging to someone else was hard to swallow. I also didn't like losing the freedom to go out when we wanted to. Everything came right in the end and I love him to bits.

Political agent

Moody blues

One of your responsibilities as a new father is to keep an eye on your partner's moods. Although it is normal for new mothers to suffer some form of baby blues three to four days after giving birth, depression that lasts for more than two weeks needs to be taken seriously. If your partner is suffering from postnatal depression – which can last from three months up to a year in some cases – the sooner she is given help the quicker it can be brought under control. Organisations such as the

When the baby cried Sue cried, which made the baby cry even more. She'd ring me at the office and then I'd feel like crying! What a mess we were all in. It took six months to sort out. Sue wouldn't admit she had a problem.

Computer systems analyst

Association for Postnatal Illness (see Appendix IV) can offer support and advice. However, you too may need their help because new dads can also suffer from a form of post-natal depression, thought to be brought on by any number of mixed emotions and confusion over their new role and responsibilities – which is just what new mothers suffer from really.

Three in a bed

A sense of humour will sustain you in moments when, your partner having found the energy to rediscover sex, the baby starts to howl just as you are both getting to the exciting bit. When this happens it's a real 'bummer'. Your partner will be even more frustrated than you at being summoned to the lord and master's cot side. If it looks like she's going to be some time settling him, put the kettle on. A cup of tea won't make up for a night of passion, but it will help to keep ardour on the boil! In time and with patience most couples' sex lives recover. Sometimes, however, professional help is needed to get back on course. There is some excellent litera-ture readily available on relationships; walk into any good book shop and browse. Or contact Relate, which has trained and very experienced relationship counsellors throughout the UK who will be able to offer advice and support during a particularly vulnerable time in your life (see Appendix IV).

Stay-at-home dad

Although it is becoming increasingly more common for fathers to be the primary carer (some reports estimate that one in five women are now the main breadwinners and one in seven homes in Britain are looked after by a house-husband), social attitudes haven't quite caught up with this trend yet. Statutory services for children are still geared to expecting the child to have its mother in tow. Public facilities for changing babies are often placed in the public conveniences for

Watching the children grow and develop, being there when they take their first steps, tie up their shoe laces for the first time ... it's wonderful.

Househusband/teacher

women, and even the names of some play facilities (mother and toddler groups?) seem to preclude fathers from becoming involved. Society does not make it easy for fathers to switch to being full-time, or even part-time, child carers, especially in public places, but don't be put off. Those who take the step find it immensely rewarding – it certainly offers plenty of material for dinner table anecdotes.

I am a stay-at-home dad. Why does society still make an issue out of my status? Why, when I turn up at coffee mornings, am I still seen as either a freak or a saint? Talk to me as an equal. After all, dads worry about the same issues as mums – safe parks, dips in the kerbs, good pre-school groups, drugs, sex, pushchair access, chocolate and blackberry stains, drugs, sex, dust mites, Dettox vs Savlon sprays, whatever happened to neighbourliness, whatever happened to drugs, whatever happened to sex.

If social attitudes could be shifted to regard child-rearing as an important 'proper' job whether undertaken by mothers or fathers ... there might be less macho talk from drunken strangers at parties – not to mention fewer guilt-ridden mums and dads shying away from telling their partners that looking after kids all day is as tiring as any 'real' job in the office.

Robert Teed, *The Independent*, 26 March 1997

You need a lot of patience. I hadn't appreciated before how long it takes to organise yourself and a small child to get out the door.

Househusband/statistician

My daughter was six months old when I was made redundant. My partner had just returned to work after maternity leave so the transition to becoming a househusband was the obvious step in the circumstances. Knowing Frances could keep us going financially I felt pretty smug about being at home and looking after the baby on a day-to-day basis. She was responsive, funny and a real joy to be with. With her in a back-pack I would cruise the museums and galleries, with very little to worry about.

Two years on and a second child on the way I need to get back to full-time paid employment. In preparation I have been taking May to a childminder now for a few weeks. The wrench, both physically and emotionally, was very painful. I felt in some way that I had betrayed her. May however looks forward to her time with the childminder. I wouldn't have missed the experience for anything.

IT consultant

After a month of being at home all day with a tiny baby I hankered after adult company and decided to try out the local Mother and Toddler's Group. A man bringing his child to play group is not welcomed with open arms. In the six Mother and Toddler's groups, in three different areas, that I have taken Laura to over the past year and a half , there have been four men, including myself, taking their children on a regular basis. New Man has yet to materialise, it seems. Or maybe he has been scared off.

Househusband/computer analyst

Father at work

One of the pressures new fathers find themselves particularly prone to is the sense of needing to increase their earning power, sparked off perhaps by the traditional view of responsible fatherhood – earn more and move to a bigger house – as well as the extra financial considerations associated with family life. Promotion is, however, often dependent on the ability to spend long hours at work and engage in networking activities after hours – working practices that can lead to fathers being absent from home for long periods, or not being around as frequently as mothers. The result is fewer opportunities for children to build close relationships with their fathers, while fathers miss out on seeing their children grow and getting to know what makes them 'tick'. In many families fathers have no choice but to work in this way. There are, however, ways in

I looked at colleagues twice divorced and thought: I don't want to end up like that.

Advertising account manager

which fathers can compensate both themselves and their children for not being able to spend much time with each other during the week. Tips to help maintain a balance between work responsibilities, which might be helpful to the working mother as well, and home include the following:

• Being involved in looking after your child from birth helps develop a natural rapport. Apart from the obvious such as picking him up to comfort him, changing and feeding him, share with your partner the task of choosing and selecting child care – good preparation too for when you need to make decisions about his schooling.

• Show your child where you work if you can, starting with when he is a baby. Renew his acquaintance with your workplace as he grows. This helps to build a picture in his mind of where you are when you are not at home, and reminds your colleagues that you are also a father.

• Put important dates in your diary so that you never forget to mark them. Dates such as birthdays, play group, nursery and school concerts, etc. Make sure you take the time to be with him on these occasions. Plan well ahead to minimise the chances of not being able to – get a list of the year's events from the school or nursery on the first day of term.

• Write to him, frequently. Little notes left under a child's pillow or received through the post have a magical effect. What you write about is not important. J. R. R. Tolkien's book *The Father Christmas Letters* started life as a letter to his three-year-old son at Christmas and continued for over twenty years – and look where it got him …

• Take up a hobby that you can do with your child – pottery, model making or photography suggest themselves as possibilities. Children as young as three can take some decent photographs. Or go swimming together once a week.

• Read to your child, regularly. This is a wonderful opportunity to be cosy. You can disappear into the story together.

• Listen to your child when he is talking to you. Busy parents sometimes only half concentrate on what their child is saying. Not wise. Children know when you are doing this. Watching his face as he speaks to you not only means you have to give him all your attention, it enables you to catch the body language of what he is telling you – which sometimes coveys a different message to the spoken words.

• Be at home when you are at home. Leave any work you have brought home with you until the children are in bed. Ban all 'phone calls during times set aside for the family, such as the evening meal, or put the answer phone on.

I loved my job and was very good at it. But I was hopeless at saying no, or delegating. To keep on top of the work and not let my own high standards down, I frequently worked 60 hours a week. And my employer was still not happy. I resigned and went freelance. Although my finances are very dodgy at times, being freed from the constant struggle to keep my head below the parapet is priceless. And I can be around my children more.

Publicist, single parent

• Tell your child about your work. This has the twofold effect of making her feel a confidante of yours, and allows you to relieve some stress associated with your work! You can do this when you are getting ready in the mornings. As she gets older this time of the day might also be useful for letting her tell you about how she is getting on in school.

• Children don't perform to order. Try to arrive home at least two nights a week long before bed time in order to give your child a chance to tell you about her day. Better still collect her from school one day a week. By the time evening comes, for most children what happened during the day has gone from their conscious mind.

• Telephoning an older child from work (if you can) as soon as he gets in from school is a good way of giving him a chance to tell you about his day while it is all still fresh.

• Develop a tradition that you always do with or for the family, like cooking on the same night each week. As your child grows older he can shop for the meal and cook it with you. It is particularly important not to lose touch with older children, whose own social lives will take them away from family life more and more, and leave even fewer opportunities to talk.

• And don't neglect your relationship with your partner, if you have one. Spring a surprise on her from time to time to let her know how much you appreciate what she does for the family. A bunch of flowers can be all that it takes to keep romance alive. Or take her out for the evening, making any child care arrangements yourself.

CHAPTER 3

Back to work?

Before the baby is born most women, especially first-time mothers, usually intend to return to the same job. And thousands do go back after maternity leave, successfully resuming where they left off. This chapter will help to prepare you for your return and advice is also given if you decide to return at a later date.

Once the baby is born, however, nearly all agonise about whether they are doing the right thing. For some parents the thought of leaving their small baby with someone else is almost more than they can bear. But being on maternity leave offers a marvellous opportunity to review the type of work you do, and to consider an alternative type of career, perhaps one more compatible with family life. The list below is intended to give you some food for thought and to help you if you are thinking of taking a career break. It is natural to consider what your practical options are at this time and, if you decide against returning to full-time work, Chapter 4, Alternative Ways of Working, will guide you through the implications in more detail.

• If you didn't return, how easy would it be to pick up the strands of your career or type of work in later years? Could you re-enter at the same salary level?

• Could you go back to being financially dependent on your partner, if you have one? Could the family live on your partner's salary?

• What impact would your decision have on your current lifestyle, household costs, mortgage payments, car costs, etc.?

On the one hand I wanted to get back to a job I enjoyed and on the other I felt the baby needed me. I've now asked to take a year's sabbatical because I still couldn't make up my mind!

Teacher

• What impact would your decision have on your retirement pension?

Although probably the last thing on your mind when you've just had a baby, this does need some thought in the context of employment changes, and some professional advice. (See also section on Your Pensions in Chapter 4, Alternative Ways of Working.)

• If you take a career break (see Chapter 4), what are the implications for company employment benefits? For instance, the arrangement is likely to be on the basis that, although you re-enter at the same level you were at when you began your career break, during the period you are off your benefits are frozen, i.e. pension payments, length of service. In other words, your continuity of service is frozen at the point at which you started your career break and starts again when you return.

• Could any loss of income be offset against savings on travel, child care costs? These could be in the region of:
  £80–120 a week for a childminder
  £90–220 a week for a nursery
  £80–260 a week for a mother's help or nanny
  £15–50 a week for out-of-school care (depending on hours)
  £50–80 a week for a holiday playscheme.

• What about investments that your (working) partner currently holds in his name? By putting them in your name you may be able to take full advantage of your personal allowance – meaning that income up to £4,045 (1997–98 allowance) could be tax free.

• As a non-tax payer, you will also accrue bank or building society interest as gross – so long as you remember to inform them of your new status.

• Could you use the time to retrain, follow a course of study that might lead to another form of employment that is easier to combine with raising a family, or set the wheels of self-employment in motion? For example, if you are a good cook, secretary or seamstress, it is possible to turn these talents into a business – with the right advice, attitude and business training. Or an Open University course might enable you to train as a teacher. (See Training Opportunities later in this chapter.)

• Or maybe you could look for work closer to home – cutting down on travel time and enabling you to be around the children more.

My partner left me just before my daughter was born. Looking back I don't know how I worked while she was very little. I certainly remember feeling very hard up financially and in a perpetual state of exhaustion. But I'm glad I stuck at it. I am about to be promoted to a more senior position and I would never have got this far if I had stopped working.

Secretary

We had just bought a bigger house when I found out I was pregnant. It wasn't planned. I had always intended to stop work for a bit when I started a family. The bigger mortgage meant I couldn't. Everything was OK in the end though. Julia is now at school and we're planning to have a second child in the next year. This time I want to go back part-time.

Civil Servant

Returning after pregnancy

Phased return

If you have no choice but to return to work after maternity leave, try to negotiate a phased return, especially if you are not entitled to, or can't afford to take, the full 40 weeks' leave (see Chapter 1, section on Statutory Rights). For instance, some companies are receptive to new mother employees working initially two days and building up to full hours over a month or two. Ideally, it is best to discuss this option with your employer before going on maternity leave, making sure that you get confirmation in writing.

(Employers have been known to renege on verbal agreements. If your employer fails to confirm a new arrangement in writing, confirm it yourself by sending your boss a friendly letter in which you set out your understanding of your discussion and her agreement to your return on a phased basis.)

You can of course still request a phased return after you have started your maternity leave, though the sooner you do it the more likely you are to have your request considered favourably. Avoid springing it on your employer at the last minute if you can.

Nevertheless, if an emergency crops up that prevents you returning full-time at the end of your leave, then suggest a phased return as a preferable option (for the company) to having to delay your return or not being able to go back at all. Aim to be constructive and realistic.

Before talking to your boss give careful consideration to the impact this would have on the company and your colleagues, so that you will have ready answers to the inevitable questions that you will be asked.

Getting your rhythm back

A few weeks before you are due to return, start to sharpen up your 'getting up and out to work' routine. You'll be surprised at how much of a shock to the system this can be after weeks of slopping around until you felt like getting dressed, or going back to bed for some sleep once your partner and older children have been seen on their way to work and school. Don't underestimate how long it will take you to get a small baby up, dressed, fed and round to the childminder – not if you want to arrive at work on time at any rate. This will give you an opportunity also to test out how well the teamwork between you and your partner pans out, offering a chance to go back to the drawing board to sort out hiccups in arrangements before the real stress of getting out to work dawns.

For instance, as you get the baby up, dressed and fed, and you prepare whatever needs to accompany him to the childminder, your partner prepares breakfast, puts out the rubbish, makes the sandwiches, or puts the washing in the machine. Use these weeks also to test how taking and collecting the baby from the childminder or nursery, or getting back on time to take over from the nanny, works out for each of you.

Breast-feeding

Continuing to breast-feed after you have returned to work is not easy to do, but it is possible. Being organised and having a truly effective breast pump are probably the secret of success. You need someplace private and hygienic to express milk during the day, a 'fridge for storing your milk and a cold bag for transporting home. (Rapidly cool your bottle of expressed milk with very cold water before storing.) The cold bag brick(s) can be stored in the freezer compartment until you are ready to leave. Sort out where you are going to express milk before going on maternity leave, if you can. Get your baby used to the bottle several weeks before you return to work and build up a store of frozen breast milk in case all doesn't go according to plan. Depending on star ratings, breast milk can be stored as follows:

- In a 'fridge for five hours.
- For up to two weeks in a freezer compartment.
- For up to four months in a deep freezer.

The Association of Breastfeeding Mothers, National Childbirth Trust, the La Leche League and Maternity Alliance may be able to offer you support and advice (see Appendix IV). Be sure to contact them long before you go back to work so you are well prepared for what is involved.

A new woman

Out with a bump, back flat as a pancake – that won't be the only difference in you when you return to work. You will be carrying all the baggage of motherhood before you. Colleagues will be wondering about your new status, and what impact it will have on your ability to do the job or your relationship with them – especially if you return on a flexible working basis. You may be feeling somewhat out of touch with workplace developments and the lives of your colleagues – the stuff of day-to-day communication, or desperately missing your baby. It may be a hard time for you, which you might have to brazen out. You will quickly prove to your colleagues that childbirth didn't cause you to lose your brain!

As soon as possible, go to lunch with the best communicator in the department and get them to bring you up-to-date with everything that's happened while you've been off. (Even if you have been in touch during your leave you will almost certainly have missed out on office gossip!)

Remember, you don't have to shut out your home life completely, so don't be afraid to put photographs of your new family on your desk. Why should you pretend they don't exist? Acknowledge it if you are missing your child, at least to friends and family. But don't go on about it, or colleagues will think that you are not committed to your work. You might find that colleagues too have changed in your absence. Some may have been promoted or new ones joined. You will have no control over these types of changes, but being prepared for them and taking the initiative with regard to your own position, i.e. by not being reticent in establishing that you are back to pick up the reins again, will help you settle back in more quickly during this potentially stressful, confidence-testing period.

Feelings of guilt

Working mothers especially are notorious for feeling guilty about being at work, mainly because they think they should be at home with their children. This is not helped by the occasional news headline about a child being harmed by a carer. Loving parents are easy prey for the doom and gloom merchants. Child care other than mother care does not harm children, and that's official. The studies on emotional attachment conducted by Dr John Bowlby more than forty years ago are still trotted

When there is not an abuse of day care, when its quality is good and parents are able to establish warm relationships with their children coming back home, positive outcomes may be found. Both my son and my grandchild attended a good day care centre, and have grown well.

Dario Varin, Professor of Developmental Psychology, State University of Milan, *The Guardian*, 24 September 1996 out as proof that a mother's place is in the home with her children. But no-one ever remembers to point out that Dr Bowlby later revised his theories to say that what made children secure and confident was the quality of care on offer, not the period spent apart from their mothers as such.

A comprehensive review of the evidence recently published in the *Journal of Child Psychology and Psychiatry* noted, in particular, that day care was unlikely to be damaging for two-year-olds, although the jury was still out about the effect on children under a year who spent more than twenty hours a week in a nursery. Furthermore, an American study concluded that children who received a good nursery education were five times less likely to become delinquent, and three times more likely to own their own houses when they grew up. The key to good child care arrangements lies in being vigilant when choosing your child's carer and not letting work keep you away from him too much.

All mothers who wanted a career or a life outside of child care worried about comments like Bowlby's: 'Mother-love in infancy and childhood is as important for mental health as are vitamins and proteins for physical health'. Then came the book that argued the primary care-giver need not be the mother, nor were her absences always hazardous – Maternal Deprivation Reassessed, *published in 1972 by Sir Michael Rutter, Professor of Child Psychiatry at London University's Institute of Psychiatry. My mother left us for a year to finish her PhD in Britain when my brother and I were both under 10. It is Rutter's book which ensured she never felt guilty for temporarily leaving us, and which ensures that, today, my wife continues her career as an eye-surgeon, as well as having children. By challenging what we believe constitutes good parenting,* Maternal Deprivation Reassessed *has changed not just my life, but all our lives.*

Dr Raj Persaud, consultant psychiatrist, The Maudesley Postgraduate Psychiatric Teaching Hospital, University of London, *The Guardian*, 21 January 1997

Returning after a number of years

Returning to the workplace, after taking a number of years out, can be a daunting business. Technology will have moved on since you were last in the office; you could find yourself being managed by someone many years younger than you, and being paid a not very attractive salary. As a first step for preparing to return, draw up a list of all your skills and experience acquired before and since becoming a mother. You'll be amazed at what this throws up. Side by

Table example of list of skills and experience as a mother

What you do	*What is involved*	*Skill*
Feed the family	Shop	Forward planning
	Cook	Budgeting
		Creativity
		Initiative
Class rep	Organise school outings	Organisation
		Marketing
	Liaise between parents and class teacher	Communication
		Negotiation
		Diplomacy
	Attend meetings	Minute taking
Course of study	Research	Critical analysis
	Writing essays	Working under pressure
	Presenting seminars	Public speaking
	Completing assignments	Meeting deadlines
		Multi-tasking

side with 'professional' skills and experience, list everything you do as a mother and any training or study you undertook while being at home. Say what this involves and then translate it into a 'workplace' skill.

The exercise is good to do even if you are returning to the same job after an extended career break. It is a good way of bolstering your confidence and reminding yourself of the value of the work you did while you were at home. It is, however, just a small part of preparing yourself for a return to work after a long time away from the workplace.

Getting some career advice and training increases your chances of finding a job that gives you satisfaction and a decent salary. If you can afford a session with a careers adviser and/or the time to follow a course of training contact the Women Returners' Network for advice. In addition, a workshop on self-esteem could help boost a low confidence for the round of interviews ahead.

Training opportunities

Your local library and Training and Enterprise Council (TEC) or Local Enterprise Company (LEC) are also good sources of information about training opportunities. To help with training costs you may be eligible for a Career Development Loan, run in conjunction with four major banks – Barclays, the Co-operative, the Clydesdale and the Royal Bank of Scotland. Sums on offer range from £200 to £8,000. TECs, LECs, job centres and local careers offices can all advise about how the loan works. Undertaking work as a volunteer in the kind of field you would like to be working in can be a worthwhile way of building up your confidence and easing your way back into 'work mode'. It has even been known for volunteers to be taken on as paid staff, once they have proved how good they are.

Family opposition

The biggest hurdle of all may, however, lie in overcoming family opposition to your decision to return to work. If the children have become used to you always being there when they come home from school, and your partner has come to expect a meal ready for him when he comes through the door, your bid for independence could go unsupported. As long as you adjust for their needs so that you can still be around some of the time for them, the children will quickly adapt to the new you.

Your partner, however, may take longer to come round. He may not like the idea of your independence. Or he might

....

It gives me a real thrill to be able to pay for things out of money I have earned. I can only afford to work because Ben is now at school and I have a reasonable childminder.

Swimming teacher

When I was at home we used to argue over how to discipline our son. Now that I am back at work we seem more relaxed about everything. I think it's because we appreciate our time together more and want to make the most of it.

Retail manager

I was nearly forty when I decided to return to work, but I couldn't bear the thought of starting as the office junior. After all, I had been my own boss for the last thirteen years. I decided to study for a vocational degree in the hope that it would get me back into paid employment at something near a level befitting my mature years. It worked. My first job on graduating was picture researcher with a national newspaper.

Press officer

feel unsettled by the inevitable changes caused by you going back to work. (If you are a new mother reading this, you may be able to avoid such a reaction by not taking over total responsibility for the children and the home during your time out of paid employment, even though sometimes this may be the easiest course of action.) You may have to work hard for your partner's support and backing, or you might just have to accept that it is not forthcoming. In which case get yourself some domestic help and make sure the children do their bit.

CHAPTER 4

Alternative ways of working

··

At different stages of life it isn't uncommon for people to take stock of their lives, maybe change their jobs, reassess their values. Becoming a parent is one of those stages. No longer able or willing to travel abroad frequently or regularly stay away from home overnight on business, or work increasingly long hours, parenthood is often the catalyst to change the working habits of a lifetime. Look around for a new job by all means if the one you have is not family friendly, but you don't necessarily have to leave your present job in order to make changes.

Those who become parents as the 1990s draw to an end and we head towards the millennium are reaping the benefits of increasing employer awareness that they can no longer afford to lose, or burn out, trained and experienced people: a company's greatest asset. As long as the approach is businesslike, many employers are now open to ideas and suggestions from employees that enable them to find a balance between employment responsibilities to the company and devoting time to family life. In fact even those

> *Don't be seduced by 24-hour canteens. You may be paid more, but the company is buying your soul. It is a grotesque lack of imagination that leads people to think that the only way they can get ahead is by working every hour of the week.*
>
> Partner, firm of City stockbrokers, lecturing MBA graduates at the London School of Business

without families are now encouraged, and want, to lead more balanced lives.

Someone who spends all their time in the same place and with the same people is unlikely to bring new and different ideas to bear on their work: companies have woken up to

I have heard colleagues say: 'I'm working hard now so I'll have time to get to know my grandchildren.' Pathetic! These are people who pride themselves on their intellectual prowess but who have not the wit to organise themselves a decent balanced life.

City investment banker

this. This chapter looks at types of flexible working practices currently in use in many areas of British industry and the implications of changing your work pattern. They are offered as suggestions to help you find your own solutions for your own particular circumstances, perhaps by using a combination, using them as short-term measures or to make changes on a more permanent basis.

. . . .

Flexible work and its implications

Your pension

As many flexible work options involve working less than full-time, contemplating a move in that direction calls for careful consideration of the financial implications, and the effect on pensions in particular. It is not widely appreciated for instance that in order to receive the full state pension you have to have paid National Insurance Contributions for a full 39 years – financial years, 1 April to 31 March. Less than this and your pension is scaled down considerably. (Even a five-year gap in employment can reduce your pension fund on retirement by between a fifth and a third, according to the financial services group Flemings.)

With women being generally less well paid than men, many, especially those in low paid, part-time and casual jobs, are unable to build up a private pension. (Parliamentary discussion is currently under way to change the pensions system radically. However, any changes are not likely to come into force until we are into the millennium. Something that has already been decided is that couples who divorce after the year 2000 will be able to split their pension rights 50:50. Try to ensure that you always get professional advice on critical financial matters.)

It is also not widely known that some people who stay at home to look after children have their Basic State Pension safeguarded even though they do not pay NICs. Since 6 April 1978, for every full tax year that a parent spends at home raising a family the state safeguards their basic pension rights with something called Home Responsibility Protection (HRP).

Briefly, it works like this: parents who take time out from paid employment to raise a family, who do not pay reduced-rate NICs and who get Child Benefit as the main payee for a child under 16 qualify under the current rules of the scheme. Those in work but who do not pay enough full-rate NICs to count towards Retirement Pension also qualify for protection.

Clearly, pensions are an area that calls for specialist advice. The following questions could be asked:

• What can you expect in the way of a state Retirement Pension if you stop work for x number of years? You can request a forecast based on your current earnings and accrued contributions by writing to the Benefits Agency, enclosing your National Insurance number (see Appendix IV).

• What impact would less than full-rate NICs have on your Retirement Pension, e.g. if you worked part-time? You should be able to work this out from your forecast, or with the help of a financial adviser.

• If you stop working or reduce your hours (hence your income) what are the implications on your private pension plan? (You are not allowed to contribute to a pension when you have no earned income.)

• Can you make up lost pension payments on returning to work or increasing your hours at a later date?

• Is there another form of savings to which you could contribute to compensate you for your lost pension earnings? Or could your (working) partner do so on your behalf?

• Is there a particular point in the tax year when it might be more beneficial to return?

Financial gains and losses

Taking a cut in salary doesn't necessarily mean that the family budget is automatically reduced by that amount. There may be cost savings attached to being at home more. For example, savings on child care, travel, office lunch costs, a reduction in the amount of expensive convenient foods most working parents resort to during the week, less drinking in the pub after work, etc. To help decide how much better or worse off a decision to take a break or work fewer hours would make you, make three lists:

1 ▶ Your current outgoings.
   ▶ Potential future outgoings – such as private education for the children, school outings, school journeys, extra activities outside school hours, holidays, etc.

2 ▶ Your current income.

   ▶ Savings made on child care, travel, food and socialising, etc. and by reducing the quantity of convenience food stuffs busy working parents tend to buy.

3 ▶ Finally look at whether you can invest for the future in any way to help counteract increased expenditure as the children get older and as insurance for you. Seek advice about insurance protection in general, for you and your family.

It may be worth noting that, according to research conducted in 1992, for the Centre for Economic Policy Research (London), a mother of two, taking a break from paid employment until the youngest child reaches school age, suffers lifetime loss of earnings of £224,000! The study assumed she took eight years out, returned on a part-time basis and lost out on salary increments and promotion. Another interesting statistic is the estimated cost of replacing a wife, thought by Legal & General to be in the region of £16,265 a year. This was arrived at by including the following per week: cooking costs of £73.31; cleaning £59.45; housekeeping £93.85; child care £43.74; driving children to school and social activities £15.37; gardening £11.03; seamstress £7.50; other chores £8.55. Although you may still opt to reduce your hours or take time out from employment, looking at all the implications before arriving at your decision leaves you free to get on and enjoy your life now, secure in the knowledge that there are no nasty surprises ahead.

If you don't have a financial adviser consult your local Citizen's Advice Bureau. The Fawcett Society may be able to let you know what the current

As a self-employed salesman I have to fit my work hours around my children. My biggest fear is what will happen to them if I become ill or have an accident.

Single father

legislation on pensions is, and perhaps recommend a financial adviser (see Appendix IV). Or call IFA Promotion on
0117 9711177 for a list of independent financial advisers in
your area.

Reduced hours

Despite the fact that people of all levels now work part-time
the phrase still has connotations of low pay, low status, lack
of commitment and reduced career prospects attached to it.
It is probably better therefore to talk in positive terms of
choosing to 'downshift' rather than 'looking for part-time
work'. If job sharing doesn't appeal to you, take a look at
how you could do the work you currently do in fewer hours.
Options might include:

• Starting later and finishing earlier, say 9.30am to 3.30pm
(giving you a thirty-hour week, allowing for a lunch hour).

• Working a four or four and a half day week, such as having every Monday off or finishing early every Friday.

• Or a nine-day fortnight – which lets you take a set day off
every other week, on a rota basis if colleagues are also on
the same system. Some
companies, however,
insist on compressing all
the contracted hours into
the nine-day fortnight by
working longer hours
each day.

*Although in effect I haven't reduced
my hours, working four longer days
a week means I can pick one son up
from nursery and the other from
school every Friday.*

Engineer

Job share

Splitting your job so that it becomes suitable for sharing
with someone else can be a very attractive proposition, for

you and your employer. You get to keep your job and work reduced hours, while your employer keeps a valued employee. Basically, job sharing amounts to dividing the responsibilities and tasks of one full-time post so that it becomes two part-time positions. Pay and benefits are pro rata, as are annual leave and bank holidays. It is possible in a job share to work split days, split weeks or alternate weeks, building in a handover period when both are present. Getting company agreement to a new working arrangement will often depend on getting the co-operation of colleagues, so be sure that you give careful consideration to how you could lessen any impact your decision might have on them, especially any you manage. Questions to ask yourself when considering this option include:

• Can you afford the reduction in your income? This could, however, possibly be offset against savings on child care costs, travel, etc.

• Could you work with someone who works differently to you? Perhaps is more or less organised?

• Does your job lend itself to splitting? For instance, does it have clearly defined tasks and responsibilities? Is it multitasking in nature? Is it fairly self-governing?

• Would the job benefit from more than seven hours a day coverage?

If you have answered yes more often than no you stand a good chance of being able to set up a job share. In selling the idea to your boss point out the gains of a job share, such as the following:

• The work is always covered, even during holiday times and periods of illness – it is common for one half of a job share to cover for the other.

• Two people give the company access to more skills and ideas for not much more than the cost of one.

• Job sharers can become very supportive of each other, often reflected in higher quality of work.

• Any initial increase in administration costs will be offset against savings on staff turnover, advertising, recruitment and work continuity.

If the concept is a new one to your company these are the sorts of contractual good practices you need to be aware of. They are not definitive and it would be wise to seek further advice from a specialist organisation such as New Ways to Work (see Appendix IV).

Contractual issues

• Each person should have a contract of employment and job description.

• Each of you should receive training as though you were full-time.

• Supervision, management and communication channels should be clearly stated.

• Each job sharer should be eligible for the company's pension scheme, sick pay, redundancy pay, maternity pay and leave, etc.

• Your contract should give you the option of returning to full-time work if your colleague leaves. If you choose not to you should help select a replacement.

A word of caution: job sharing is not necessarily the antidote to stress that it is sometimes held up to be. Although there are many examples of very successful team partnership job shares, they can also have their drawbacks, for instance one partner covering up for the inefficiency of the other. Or packing four days work into your two and a half. Think about what you want in a partner before entering an agreement. And be very honest and direct with each other from the outset, airing disagreements as soon as they occur.

Flexi-time

This is a system widely used in the Civil Service, Local Authority and charity sectors, but less so in other areas of employment. It works by letting employees choose their own start and finish time, though companies usually stipulate being at work during core hours – commonly between 10am and 4pm. Hours worked are recorded and added up at the end of agreed periods of settlement – usually one month. Characteristically, flexi-time arrangements include the following:

• Lunch breaks of no less than 30 minutes and no more than one and a half hours.

• An agreed number of hours carried over to the next month, not more than 10 usually.

• A formal logging system, ranging from signing in and out on a special form kept by a supervisor to computerised networks.

Flexi-time can be useful for organising working life around family needs, although employees on flexi-time need to guard against working more hours than they are paid for.

I always make sure I pick the children up from school one day a week. I leave the office at 1pm, taking work with me to do later in the evening when they are in bed.

Project manager, father of three

77

Shift working

Although not ideal for family relationships shift work can be a solution to the question of child care, especially if costs are high. Mother can be home during the day, with father taking over when she goes to work in the evening, or vice versa. However, it only works if both parents are living together and share all responsibilities pretty evenly. Indeed shift work can be a nightmare for single parents. What, for instance, is the nurse who goes on duty at 8am and finishes at 8pm supposed to do with children who start school at 9am and finish at 3pm? In some circumstances not a particularly good option then. But in others it can work quite well.

I recently changed from doing the night shift to an evening shift and I am much less tired than I used to be. I now work from 5.30pm to 10pm which means I can be with the children during the day.

There's very little time for us as a couple though as I am often on duty at weekends too.

Mother of four-year-old twins, doctors' answering service

Term-time working

This allows parents to be off during the school holidays. Teachers are the obvious group of employees able to take advantage of this form of employment, but the retail and factory sectors also offer it. Contracts either allow employees to take unpaid leave during the school vacation period or make it possible for employees to spread their annual salary across twelve months.

I share the children's nanny with another family. She looks after their children in the school holidays which means I don't have to find the money to pay her salary when I really don't need her.

Teacher

Annual hours

Previously associated with the manufacturing industry, other employers have also begun to implement yearly contracts, perhaps because of a need to reduce working hours overall or to control overtime.

A number of hours for the whole year are written into your contract, allowing you to plan for seasonal peaks and troughs. Some compan-

I save up my leave and take it all together during the school summer holidays.

NHS speech therapist, single parent

ies split the total number of hours into two parts, the greater number being worked in set times and the rest left unallocated to be used by mutual agreement. You have to guard against being asked to cover for colleagues at short notice and doing more than your contracted hours. It may not be flexible enough to meet the needs of a young family.

Working from home

This is a broad term encompassing the self-employed and those who work for an employer from home, and is sometimes called telecommuting. There are many excellent books on the market entirely devoted to the particular requirements of self-employment, so I am not proposing to reinvent the wheel. Before passing on, however, and speaking as someone who is self-employed, it can be an option well worth considering. In addition to reading up on the subject, your local Training and Enterprise Council (TEC), known as Local Enterprise Companies (LECs) in Scotland, will be able to give you advice about setting up, training and any grants available to you.

Here I use the term 'working from home' to mean working for an employer but based at home, occasionally or much of the time. According to a recent report in the London *Evening Standard* (24 March 1997) over three million people are expected to work from home by the year 2000; almost one in three employees expects to be able to work from home within the next fifteen years, the benefits of which include:

• Teleworking could save a central London company with 100 staff around £2 million a year in transport and office costs alone.

• Working from home would save UK drivers 142 million car trips a week.

Information technology has opened up a vast array of jobs to being done at home, if not full-time then at least part of the time. Take a look at what you do and how you do it. Do you really need to be on your employer's premises in order to do it? If all it would take to enable you to work from home is some organisation, goodwill – on the part of your boss – and some computer equipment, then go for it. To work from home, you will need to follow the points below:

• Have clear objectives about what the job entails.

• Set realistic targets about when objectives can be met.

• Hold regular meetings with your boss.

• Be self-disciplined and motivated.

• Keep in frequent touch with colleagues.

• Have an area set aside as an office, cut off from the ordinary day-to-day business of the home.

• Make rules about when you are available to the children and where they are able to play rowdy games while you are working.

• Make rules about how the 'phone is answered and messages recorded – though this can largely be taken care of by installing a business line.

• Make sure that deadlines and targets are always met, or give plenty of warning that the schedules have proved to be unrealistic and deadlines/targets need to be reset to those on whom they will impact.

All these points are musts for successful home working. Although you will almost certainly still need to make some form of child care arrangements for babies and small children, you will at the very least save on travel time and costs, while the company saves on office overhead costs. (Insurance may be something you need to watch if you take up this option. Check whether you are covered under your company's policies and ask the advice of your own household insurers.)

Zero hours

A practice common in the retail and service sectors is for employers to call on a registered pool of staff as and when they are required. Not a great option for someone trying to earn some money and look after a family. It is difficult to predict when you might be offered some work, and so it is hard to make child care arrangements in advance. Another drawback is the lack of employment benefits and rights inherent in this form of work.

Career break

If none of the above appeals or is possible for you to do, but you are miserable at the thought of returning to work while your child is little, is there anything else you can consider?

If your company operates a career break scheme and you can afford to take lengthy unpaid leave, then this could be the best option of all – giving you the security of the option to return to a job while at the same time leaving you free to explore a change of direction. The length of time off varies from company to company and can be anything from one to five years. As career breaks are mostly discretionary, your company may not be broadcasting the fact that it offers this option. Check with your personnel department, or whoever is responsible for staff matters in your organisation. If not, ask to discuss the possibility of taking one anyway. Read again the opening section of Chapter 3, Back to Work?, when considering the implications of taking a career break.

Typically, companies tend to have a set of criteria attached to career breaks, such as a minimum amount of service, a commitment to return and working a number of weeks each year in order to keep in touch and maintain skills – sometimes to cover for colleagues on holiday. Check the fine print to see how safe your job is while you are off; you won't necessarily be guaranteed to get it back when you return. Make sure that you are also clear about the effects on your employment benefits, pension and long service record, etc. Check with your personnel department, or equivalent, and ask them to clarify the terms in writing (see also Chapter 3, Back to Work?).

I gave up a good career to look after my children. Now that I want to go back to work it seems employers aren't interested in people who have been out of the workforce for more than a year. Running a home requires far more organisational ability than the average job. Employers just don't realise what a valuable asset conscientious mothers are.

Former police officer

Formalities and legalities

If you reduce your hours, salary, leave and benefits should be calculated on a pro-rata basis. In this respect the Equal Pay Act, court case precedent and House of Lords rulings have ensured that those working part-time now qualify for the same employment rights and protection as full-time employees. In addition, an employer who refuses to allow a mother to reduce her hours on returning from maternity leave may be guilty of unlawful discrimination – in the same way as it would be to refuse a man's request to reduce his hours on the grounds of his sex. However, even though your family commitments may grant you the legal right to reduce your hours (not a foregone conclusion) many managers hold the view that part-time working is problematic for them, so you could still meet with resistance.

I have two daughters aged eight and ten. As a single parent I felt it was important to be able to spend at least some time with them during the week. I work three days a week which means I can pick the girls up from school on the other two. Keeping afloat financially is a constant battle. But we manage.

Shop assistant

Approaching your boss

Managers get used to having their staff around them all the time and members of staff who work less than a full week, or partly from home, call for new thinking about the way that they are managed and supervised. In the current climate of job insecurity, almost perpetual corporate restructuring and job overload, managerial reluctance to give themselves yet another (perceived) problem is understandable. To break down his or her resistance you will need to sell your boss a sound business case about the benefits of part-time working – one of which could be that the alternative is to lose you completely.

At first I was frightened about whether I really could do my job in three days but I am staggered by how much I get done. I'm much more focused and organised and I still seem to get the same amount done. Makes me wonder how much time I wasted before!

Head of Human Relations

Your proposal should cover the implications from every angle – and especially the company's, as those are the ones that are going to interest him most. He will need convincing that his life won't be made more difficult by making yours easier! In winning him over, suggest that you both give the new arrangement a trial period, say for four months. This gives you time to win his trust and prove that being part-time is no less productive than full-time and, in fact, it is often the reverse.

Part-time workers tend to come to work more refreshed, full of energy, get on with what they have to do, and go. There is no procrastination, or stopping for cups of coffee or chats by the coffee machine. Seek out colleagues who already work less than full-time and pick their brains about the problems they had and how they overcame them. Alternatively, contact New Ways to Work for advice on putting a convincing case to your boss, and perhaps to be put in touch with other part-timers in your field. For advice on your legal position, consult the Equal Opportunities Commission Work and Family Unit (see Appendix IV).

I know my staff work too many hours and I fear their social lives are suffering. I recognise their commitment, but I admire them more when they say 'enough is enough'.

Roger Young, Institute of Management, *The Guardian*, 1 March 1997

Winning over your colleagues

Consider too the likelihood of opposition from colleagues. Even if your decision has no direct impact on them, they are likely to feel a bit resentful at the thought of you leading the life of Reilly at home, while they are slaving over hot desks. Once your new arrangement has been agreed, in principle, canvas their views and take their concerns into account when finalising the arrangement. For example, suppose you want to do a four-day week: try to make your day off the one that causes the least inconvenience to your colleagues.

If, despite all your endeavours, your colleagues still mutter about special treatment, put them right on a few facts, such as it is today's children, tomorrow's workers, who will pay for their pensions and services in their old age. The trail you blaze now can only be to their advantage in the long run; family-friendly policies and practices are often the forerunners of better employment conditions for everyone.

In fact there are signs that this is happening in the USA, where many companies have already implemented Employee Assistance Programmes (EAPs) to help combat the high levels of stress that their employees are experiencing. EAPs offer a package of support measures, such as family counselling, career guidance, child care advice, etc., designed to help individuals balance their lives better. EAPs are also used to monitor and influence corporate culture.

The impetus for changing corporate culture in the USA came from employees themselves, many of whom took the conscious decision to 'downshift' in an effort to reduce their stress levels. The effect of losing many highly trained specialist people caused companies to question the role that they played in the lives of their employees. Often a little behind the USA on these issues, EAPs are now beginning to find favour with companies in the UK.

The business case

There is a great deal of evidence around now to show that family friendly packages benefit employers. It is hardly surprising really since employees who feel valued and respected will naturally have greater commitment and experience deeper job satisfaction. For example, a recent study, commissioned by Allied Domecq and the Government Office for the West Midlands, of the impact of family-friendly practices on firms concluded that:* 'Private sector companies considered that enhanced personnel practices improved business performance.'

• Two-thirds of the companies surveyed reported increased profitability.

If you punish people for putting family first, you end up with a bunch of ambitious nutters, when what you need is balanced people.

Sir John Harvey-Jones, former chairman of ICI

• Eight out of ten reported higher productivity, one commenting: one product in particular has improved from thirty days' production to only four days.

• Lower production costs or reduced wastage were experienced by sixty-one per cent of businesses – primarily because jobs were done more accurately, with less need to do something a second time. (Implies employees were more committed and experienced greater job satisfaction.)

• Eighty-three per cent of respondents reported greater overall customer satisfaction.

I am prepared to work 60-hours a week, but I am not prepared to let work take over my life.

28-year-old final year MBA graduate

* Study carried out by Prism Research. Source: *Shropshire Star*, 13 March 1997 and Shropshire Chamber of Commerce.

But it may fall to you to make your employer aware of the benefits. Organisations such as Parents At Work, Employers For Childcare, Opportunity 2000 and the Industrial Society can all provide you with the facts.

Preparing your proposal

Dissect your job to see where and how it can be adapted to flexible working – start with your job description:

- Draw up a list of pros and cons looking at:
  - why it would be good and bad for you
  - the impact of your decision on your employer and your colleagues
  - how any problems that arise from doing your job differently can be overcome. For example, if you want to downshift to four days a week try to take your day off at the quietest time, being on hand to cover for the busiest periods.

- Take a business-like approach, adopting whatever is appropriate for your own setting. For instance, do you present a formal written proposal or is it sufficient to have a meeting with your boss? If the latter, it is always good practice to follow it up by putting your understanding of the outcome of the meeting in writing. That way you won't run into the possibility of your boss forgetting he agreed to something at a later stage.

- There are bound to be some disadvantages all round, but the benefits may outweigh them. Look to emphasise the positive. For instance, would you have to give up work entirely if you can't reduce your hours? In which case it is in everyone's interest to find a compromise to prevent this. The company can keep trained and experienced personnel, your commitment to it is increased and you maintain your earning power.

• Dropping in the odd statistic about cost savings is a powerful way of making your boss take notice of the business advantage. At a recent British conference, Rank Xerox estimated that its equality measures had brought it a return of £1 million over five years through savings on staff retention, recruitment and production. Glaxo Wellcome maintained that an employer child care scheme paid for itself when set against the cost of replacing staff who would otherwise have had to resign.

Reviewing the situation as your children grow

As your children move from one phase to another, such as starting primary and secondary school, you may need to review your working arrangements to fit in with their needs. What works when children are very little may not be suitable for older children, for instance. Try to keep your work life flexible enough to allow you to keep in touch with your children's lives and interests. But in particular, make a point of getting the complete list of school holidays, open days, events, etc., on the first day of the school year. Armed with this you can plan for those times when you will need to make alternative child care arrangements, as well as for all those times when it will be important to your children that you are there, such as, school visits, school concerts, meetings with teachers, school fêtes, doing the rounds of schools when changing from primary to secondary.

As soon as the children got to school age we resolved to spend as much of the summer as we could and the whole of the Easter and half-term holidays as a family. We are both lucky to have employers who are flexible enough to let us do this. It means of course taking a lot of unpaid leave.

Statistician, father of three

CHAPTER 5

Dealing with stress

At work

At a time when lifetime employment can no longer be assumed, holding on to precious jobs becomes a full-time occupation in itself. Job insecurity and financial pressures have seen a rise in the numbers of people doing what amounts to the work of two, even three, people. Although not the only causes of work-related stress, work overload and its companion, long working hours, are two of the major ones. Others are poor work relationships, feeling unappreciated or undervalued, lack of job satisfaction, awkward journeys to and from work, and change, either to a new job or new department, or simply returning to the workplace after maternity leave. For working parents, workplace stress is compounded by the perennial battle to keep work pressures from spilling over to the home and vice versa.

Nobody eliminates stress completely from their life, indeed a certain amount keeps the adrenaline flowing and the senses sharp. Dealing successfully with stress means identifying the causes and developing coping strategies to reduce it to a safe level. Chapter 4 on Alternative Ways of Working looked at options for reducing work hours; this chapter

When I can get home in time to read my kids a bedtime story, there is nothing better for me.

Long distance lorry driver

looks at other common causes of stress, with suggestions about how they might be minimised. They may provide useful insights into the causes of stress, and help you to identify and cope with yours.

When I finally plucked up the courage to tell my boss that my workload had got out of hand, I ended up feeling sympathy for her! We sat for about half an hour chewing the cud and commiserating with each other, 'we were both just cogs in a wheel and nobody cared about us', that sort of thing. I still ended up with the same workload but I felt more supported by my boss after that. Made things a bit more bearable.

Local government officer

Work overload

Realistically you will probably have limited control over your workloads, but that shouldn't stop you trying to have more. Often we are our own worst enemies, taking on more than we should and then feeling angry about it. If your boss assigns you yet another task on top of a pile you are already struggling to get through, put the decision about what gets done when back on her desk. Decide how long it is going to take you to do each piece of work, task or project. Set them out as a list, then go to your boss and ask for her help to list them in order of priority.

To help you have a positive attitude of mind before you go to see your boss, leave any feelings of resentments you might have in a drawer in your desk. This is a serious suggestion! Visualise your resentments in an imaginary box locked in a drawer in your desk. This will help you focus on the meeting in hand and keep you from saying something you might regret later. Conveying confidently that you know you do a good job, but you can't be expected to stand on your head as well, will earn the respect it deserves. If you can, avoid accepting or committing yourself to an agreement that would benefit from some thought. 'I'll get back to you on that' or 'I'll need to think about that' are useful phrases for buying time. By highlighting how overworked you are you also put paid to any notion that you simply aren't up to the job. You may, however, need to repeat the exercise at frequent intervals.

My boss would swan in around three o'clock in the afternoon, hand me a pile of correspondence and documents for typing then expect me to make the four o'clock post. No matter how fast I typed I never managed to get everything out in time. I felt such a failure. Then I realised that I wasn't the problem. After that I started to train my boss to fit in with my schedules. I would give her a list of what I had to do the next day and add that if she had anything urgent she should get it to me before one o'clock. It worked.

Stockbroker's secretary

Unsupportive colleagues

Inevitably, working parents just have to curtail the number of hours spent at work. If there is a child to be collected from the childminder or after school club, come collecting time you, or your partner, have to be there. Unfortunately, colleagues sometimes resent working parents for seemingly leaving 'early' or working flexibly. Uppermost in their minds is the thought that if they are still there when you leave then they must be working harder than you. Not true at all, of course. This is misplaced resentment which fails to recognise that the problem lies not with working parents but with skewed working practices. Unsupportive colleagues are a symptom of high stress levels. And resentment in itself is of course another cause of stress. It is more constructive to look at why everyone is spending excessively long hours at work, and what can be done to reduce them. As has been said elsewhere in this book, accepting the status quo is not necessarily your only option.

When I was first a working parent I nearly killed myself proving I could be successful at my job and keep the most perfect home. Now I am much more laid back about the way the house is. But I have never carried that attitude over to my work. I wouldn't give my colleagues the satisfaction of saying my children interfered with being able to do a good day's work.

Teacher, mother of three

Workplace support group

One way of tackling resentment and a generally poor working environment is to explore the notion of setting up a workplace support group, if there isn't one on site already. Joining or setting up a workplace support group can bring parents together to share information, pass on tips, form child care networks and friendships, offer reassurance when

. . . .

I returned to work when my son was three and a half months old. I felt ghastly but we couldn't afford for me to take more time off. There seemed very little understanding or support for a newly returned Mum. Colleagues had a changed attitude towards me, after all, I was a mother now! I was missing my son and contact with other mothers. If I was feeling this way maybe others were too. It was then I decided to set up a Working Parents Group. During the year that we have been established the company has radically altered its maternity policy, introduced the right to return on a part-time basis and consults the group about broader personnel issues.

Geologist

times are difficult, take the place of neighbourhood support groups and be a force for positive change in the workplace. Setting one up isn't difficult to do, though a certain amount of organisation is involved to get it off the ground. The effect on the working environment, however, can be tremendous. To talk to people who have already benefited from one and for advice on how to set one up contact Parents At Work, Opportunity 2000 and Employers For Childcare (see Appendix IV).

Office meetings

Meetings that start very early in the morning or begin late afternoon are the scourge of working parents. If you are in a position to influence their timing, fix them for times that suit your family needs. If you have no control over when they

Where I work is full of people who stay late because they think it looks good. From the first day back after maternity leave I established the fact that I was going to leave at 5.30 every evening. I wanted to make it clear that I now had a very good reason for leaving on time.

Book editor

are fixed, try having a 'meeting already arranged' that you can't postpone or rearrange when you are asked to attend ones that you know are going to be hell to make on time, or raise your blood pressure by making you very late back to collect the children. If you have to come clean about your reasons for not being able to make meetings at the crack of dawn and last thing at night, do so in a positive and assertive way. Say you would love to make the meetings and feel you miss out

Senior staff have more control over their lives, but there are no Brownie points for jackets over the chair at 9pm or for hanging around at work when you don't need to be there. The message is: get a life!

Partner, firm of solicitors

by not being able to, but your family responsibilities make it impossible. Could meetings be held at other times so that you could attend?

Predicting stress and being prepared

Some situations are guaranteed to cause stress, for example, departmental meetings at which you have to give a presentation. As a working parent it is more important than ever to be well prepared for events that you can anticipate will cause you stress. The following ideas will help:

• Prepare your report or presentation far ahead; you can't afford to leave it until a day or so before. What if someone in the family were ill and you were up all night worrying and nursing them?

• Try to batch cook once a week or fortnight to avoid having to get a meal ready every evening. This also means that you can ask your teenager to pop something in the oven if you are delayed leaving the office.

• Keep your approach to work and family life flexible enough to allow you to change immediately a routine that isn't working.

• Keep on top of sleep.

The journey to work

Most people find the journey to work a great hassle. If you can't change your route or your hours to avoid the rush hour, learn how to consciously relax to help you arrive at work less stressed than when you left home. Don't catch up on office work while you travel if this only stresses you more. Try listening to a tape of relaxing music instead.

Communication skills

Being successful at getting what you want, while at the same time making everyone else feel they too are a winner, is probably the most vital of workplace skills. This involves feeling confident, being assertive

If your well-being and sense of self is totally dependent on external factors – salary, status – you may well feel vulnerable. With self-esteem you have a basic confidence in yourself that whatever happens you'll manage the situation.

Self-esteem management consultant

without being aggressive, valuing your worth and yourself, and having the ability to negotiate. As a parent you are probably practising all these skills already without realising it. To help you fine tune them for use in the workplace, you may need the help of a specialist. Look out for notices of self-esteem, personal effectiveness or negotiating skills workshops near where you live, or ask to be sent on one as part of development and training. Here are some points that can help:

- *Confidence* When you shrug off fear of being disliked or of losing your job it is easier to say no to unreasonable demands.

- *Self-esteem* When you respect and value yourself others do too.

- *Assertiveness* When you start taking responsibility for yourself and your actions you start to be assertive, which stops you feeling a victim or a martyr.

- *Negotiation* When you arrive at a compromise that has taken account of all viewpoints and left no-one feeling resentful, negotiations can be said to have been successful.

At home

If your efforts to improve your conditions at work have proved too much of an uphill struggle, focus instead on keeping all other areas of your life as stress free as possible – your home in particular. Accepting that which you can't change will already lower your stress level. While you may not be able to prevent the baby keeping you awake all night, your toddler having a tantrum, your teenage daughter dying her hair pink, the freezer packing up, the cat eating the hamster or your childminder being suddenly taken ill ... you do at least have control over how the household functions.

In many ways the home environment is no different from the workplace environment in that, to keep it running smoothly, stress must be kept to a minimum, with everyone pulling in the same direction; each member of the family has to play a part in keeping it on course. Just like in the workplace, even though working as a team is the objective, someone has to direct operations. This is where house rules come in. Decide, with your partner if you have one, what causes most conflicts then set about eliminating the sources.

Household routine

Start by drawing up a list of household chores, for example, shopping, cooking, washing up, vacuum cleaning, emptying the bin, putting the washing in the machine, hanging it up, putting it away, ironing, changing the beds, taking the papers to the paper bank, bottles to the bottle bank, putting the children to bed, delivering and

I turn a blind eye to the fact that the children are wearing odd socks and that the hoovering isn't quite how I'd like it done and let him do it his way.

Civil Servant

collecting children to and from the childminder, or wherever. Then delegate as appropriate, or find ways of easing the burden if you have only yourself to delegate to. Granted, small babies won't be able to do much, but from an early age children should be expected to play their part too, if only to take care of their own rooms.

If you extend responsibility to children for other areas of the household rotate the tasks to prevent sulking and accusations that one child is doing more than a sibling. Having a relaxed attitude to household cleaning standards will help keep your blood pressure normal. Let everyone do what they have to do to the best of their ability. Resist criticising and the urge to do it yourself because you know you would do it better. Compromise, perhaps by keeping one room clean and tidy. Or, if you can afford a cleaner, employ one (helps reduce the need to nag the family to do their bit) and have everything you can delivered.

After months of getting no support from my partner I finally resorted to drastic measures. I took to preparing sandwiches just for me. I stopped washing and ironing his shirts. I engaged a cleaner. I put our child on his side of the bed when he cried at night. I stopped short at leaving the baby permanently with the childminder! He eventually got the message.

Working mother of two

Tension seekers

Anticipate times when tension is likely to be at its highest: early morning when parents are getting ready to go to work, and children plus their baggage have to be organised to be taken to the childminder or to school, and end of day mealtimes and getting the children to bed tend to be the two most common periods. Plan ahead for known fraught times, for example, sort out the night before what the children need to take with them the next day.

I remember dashing to make a train in the morning, dashing to make a train in the evening, sprinting up to the front door at night then standing outside for ten minutes while I tried to get into Postman Pat mode.

Chief executive

If you have school-age children, check whether they have any notes from school that need to be acted upon immediately – such as the school has to close for the day unexpectedly! Give the children some responsibility for getting out the door on time by asking them to lay out the clothes that they want to wear the night before. (If he wants to wear summer shorts in the middle of winter try to get him to wear a number of underpants and knee high socks!)

Child care

Other high stress triggers for working parents are conflicts with carers, arrangements that fall apart or let you down, feeling jealous of the relationship your child has with his carer or having to take time off to be with a sick child. When child care works, everything in the garden is rosy. When it doesn't it affects your ability to work. Read Chapter 6 on Child Care Options for a comprehensive overview of all aspects of child care, including how to make it work and installing a safety net for those times when it doesn't.

The week before I was due to go back to work my child care arrangements fell through and my partner was made redundant. My first reaction was one of horror, then I realised that my partner being at home at least bought me time to find another nanny. He ended up looking after the baby for six months, and loved it.

Fashion buyer

Children

Worrying about whether older children are feeling neglected now that the family has a new baby to look after, coping with a child who is going through a difficult 'phase' (do children have any other kind?), dealing with sibling rivalry, having a child with special needs or trying to get to grips with teenage angst or anarchy can all cause parents a great deal of distress. Already troubled about the amount of time and attention they can give their children, when the child of a working parent is 'playing up' or unhappy, guilt goes into overdrive – it's all my fault/if only I had stayed at home/I should spend more time with the children.

I came home one night to find my daughter's boyfriend had moved in. This at a time when I was in the throes of parting from her father! I screamed at the pair of them, told my husband to sort it out, then went round to a friend and drank a good bottle of wine.

Graphic designer

You can only do your best for your children, don't expect more of yourself. All relationships go through bad patches. And whilst it is certainly true that time spent together does nurture relationships it doesn't mean that you have to give 24 hours a day to them. If in the natural course of time your child's behaviour and your relationship with her fails to improve, contact a parenting support organisation, such as Exploring Parenthood or Parent Network, for advice (see Appendix IV for details of these and other useful organisations).

Family time

Inevitably, work cuts down and impacts on family time, especially if work has to be taken home, compounding the anxieties of working parents. In reality, however, parents may have little choice but to bring work home. In any case the alternative – even longer hours spent at work and away from the family – is less preferable. There are some safeguards you can use, however, to help keep spill-over to a minimum and reduce this source of stress.

I made sure to set my colleagues' expectations that family is important to me. I used to be asked to cancel holidays at the last moment. Now I guard that time by announcing it in advance.

City bank economist

• Ban all 'phone calls, including personal ones, during times set aside for the family – between the time you get home and when the children are in bed, for instance.

• At least once a week make sure you have a meal together as a family. When you come home tired from work it is so tempting to give the children their meal, get them off to bed, then for you and your partner to have a snack as you pore over work brought home from the office. But you can very quickly lose the knack of communicating with each other this way. One morning you may wake up and realise that you have stopped knowing what makes your partner tick, lost touch with your children and you are no longer working as a team. Turn what has to be done in any case – eating – into a family social gathering and a time to catch up on everyone's news.

Because I work such odd hours we lead a very limited social life. But we always do something together at the weekends. To make sure that we make the most of our time together we plan our time very carefully, even our leisure time is mapped out.

Social worker, father of three

• Encouraging older children to take up a sport, join an organisation (such as Girl Guides or Scouts) and/or develop independent relationships with grandparents, cousins or friends is a means of providing them with their own support networks, as well as offering opportunities for holidays without the need for you to accompany them.

Me time

In a frantically busy world, compounded by being a working parent, make sure you set aside a regular period of time when you can recharge your own batteries. It doesn't have to cost money, treating yourself to a luxurious soak in a bathroom lit with candles or floating in the bath (the candles that is) can be wonderfully soothing on the nerves. Be sure that the rest of the family clearly understands that you are not to be disturbed at this time. Other relaxation tips include going swimming, taking up yoga, pursuing a hobby, going to the cinema or theatre with friends, having a massage, working-out in a gym, running round your local track, walking in the park, meeting a friend for coffee, a session in a flotation tank, anything that is time spent on you without the family around. Whatever you choose make it a regular feature of your life, once a week if you can – build it into your time management plan!

I cope by limiting what I take on. I have to feel in control of my life, and I make sure that others realise I can only do one thing at a time. I insist on a lie-in at the weekends and I have trained my children not to disturb me until they hear me up and about.

Single father of two

The perfect parents

Working or otherwise, the perfect parents have yet to be born, and there is little chance they ever will, thank goodness. How dull the world would be if we had nothing to strive for! But good planning and organisation will help you to feel good about yourself.

I'm not an organised person by nature but this has become the key to my survival. We worked out a weekday routine that we always stick to. Rob gets the baby up and dressed while I prepare breakfast and feed her. In the evening Rob cooks our meal and we both take a hand in putting the baby to bed. We never do housework during the week, apart from putting toys away and washing up. We relax and enjoy each other's company instead.

Personnel officer

CHAPTER 6

Child care options

Finding and choosing child care are probably the aspects of working parenthood that cause the most angst. But get them right and everything else falls into place.

Giving yourself plenty of time to find your Mary Poppins makes an enormous difference to the outcome. Before reading up on the various options, list everything connected with your work and home life which could influence your choice of child care arrangements, for instance:

• The time you need to leave the house by.

• The needs of your other children if this is not your first baby – their current child care arrangements, taking them to and from school, their after-school activities, social life, etc.

• Whether you can rely on a partner to share responsibility for the children.

• Whether your journey to and from work by public transport is prone to disruption.

• Meetings you have to attend which start early and finish late in the day.

A mother's education is a powerful indicator of her children's likely educational achievements, new research suggests ... having a working mother may even increase the odds that the child goes on to A-levels and beyond.

Lucy Ward, *The Independent*, March 1 1997

• Whether you have fixed holiday periods or can take them more or less as you want.

• Whether you can control the hours you spend at work.

I have been accused of shunting my child from home to childminder, to nursery, back to childminder and eventually home. But I would not exchange the caring relationship she has with her childminder for the convenience of an all day nursery place.

Part-time worker,
mother of three-year-old

• Whether you can bring work home to finish, allowing you to leave earlier/whether your company is family friendly/allows leave for family and/or domestic reasons.

• The time you normally get home.

As you work through the options, and the pros and cons of each, refer to the list and award each type of child care marks out of ten for suitability. Bear in mind, however, that your ideal option may not be available to you; you may have to settle for second or third best. Nevertheless, using the guide given in this chapter you will be reassured that your decision is an informed one. Ultimately, whatever your child care arrangements, stability and a safe caring environment are what enable children to grow into secure adults.

Childminders

Childminders have self-employed status and look after children in their own homes. Occasionally you come across a group of childminders who have formed a co-operative and are based at a local community centre. Being self-employed childminders can, and do, set their own rates of fees, hours of work, holidays, whether or not they look after children who are ill (such as with a heavy cold), etc., which allow for local variation. In the UK, the Children Act 1989 requires all childminders to register for inspection by their Local Authority Registration and Inspection Department to ensure that they meet basic criteria with regard to health and safety matters, such as the suitability of their homes for child-minding purposes; this also affects the ages and number of children a local authority will allow a childminder to care for at any one time. The usual limit is three children under five and three of school age – including the childminder's own children.

Registered childminders, and anyone else in the household who will be present at the same time as 'minded' children, also undergo a police check to see if they have any criminal record, especially relating to child abuse. In addition, quite a number of local authorities require childminders to train in basic first aid, child development and child health as part of registration. Many will also insist that the premises are inspected by Fire and Environmental Health officers.

Finding your childminder

As the registering body, local authorities maintain lists of registered childminders, so this is the obvious first place to start. Call the main switchboard, explain what you are after and ask which department you need to contact – which varies from council to council. Try to ensure that you get a specific name and direct line or extension number. Take heed at this point that it may be a tedious operation so start your quest weeks ahead of your return date. It can be diffi-cult making contact with the right person, either because they never seem to be at their desk when you wish to speak with them or because you have been given the wrong name in the first place! Perseverance is the name of the game here.

It can pay dividends to speak with the registering officer. She (it usually is a woman) will be familiar with her 'clients' in your area and may be able personally to recommend a childminder. Or she may be able to tell you of someone who is about to be registered but whose name is not on the list of names and addresses that will be sent to you, and which is sometimes out of date. By definition, someone about to be registered will be looking for customers and could be a better bet than trawling through a list of names only to discover none of them has vacancies. This is another reason for giving yourself plenty of time to find child care before it becomes a desperate need.

If you want to know about childminders in a borough other than the one in which you live – perhaps because you'd like to find one close to where you work, the procedure is the same as making contact with your own local authority. Don't be fobbed off by being told this information is available only to those who live in the borough: you have the right to be given it under the Children Act 1989.

Other ways of locating childminders in your area include contacting the National Childminding Association (see Appendix IV), asking at your local library (some councils provide this information via library computer systems), asking friends and neighbours, putting notices up in local schools, chatting to the play leader at your local mother and toddler group, often based in community centres or church halls, asking your Health Visitor.

Fees

Childminder fees vary from location to location but generally are the same throughout any one particular geographical area. Quality and experience will be the determining factor for a particular childminder's fees. You'll be able to get an idea of costs for your area from your local authority. Parents are sometimes a little stunned by childminder fees, which can start at £80 a week per child for all-day care. (Childminders will generally adjust their fees for two or more children from the same family.) You might find it helpful then to know the basis on which fees are set. Aside from time spent caring for the children childminders also have to cover themselves for wear and tear on their homes, tax and National Insurance, heating and lighting costs, public liability insurance, extra play equipment, inspection fees, lean times, etc. – in short all the things any other self-employed person has to take into consideration when setting a fee.

Making the most of interviews

Telephone to begin with to check that she has a vacancy for your child. If she doesn't currently have a vacancy for your child, but one is due to become available soon, could she keep it for you? What deposit would she want? (If the place doesn't materialise the deposit should be returned to you. Conversely, if you don't take up the place you are likely to lose your deposit.) Over the 'phone ask what hours she is available, what her fees are, length of time she has been a childminder, number of children she cares for and their ages, whether she has pets and/or smokes – both of which you might not want around your child. If you just want to reserve a place at this stage, does she charge a retainer fee?

Commonly, childminders charge half their normal fee to reserve a place, which should not be charged if there is no place available. (Similarly, your childminder should not charge you for a place if she takes a holiday outside your agreed hours.) Depending on the childminder, this fee may be returned if you decide not to take up the place. The full fee comes into operation if a place is taken up during the retaining period. A good childminder will not mind you asking these questions, they cut down on time wasting. Satisfied that you would like to proceed further arrange to visit. Try not to take your child with you on the first visit so as not to be distracted while you interview her. If you like what you find, return for a second visit, this time taking your child with you so you can watch them interact.

Quality checks

When you visit the childminder note the 'feel' of the house:

• Is it too tidy?

• Too untidy?

• Do the other children seem happy and carefree in the childminder's presence?

• Are there pictures by the children on the walls?

Watch how she is with the other children:

• Does she give them her attention when they look for it?

• Ask whether she enjoys her work, what type of child care training she has and whether she is trained in first aid.

• Ask her to describe what a typical day for her and the children would be like.

• Does she take them out?

• Where do they go?

• How does she get there?

• Does she provide meals?

• What do you provide in the way of clothing, nappies, money for trips out, etc.?

Ask how she sees your child fitting in with the other children – especially if the other children are much older. Would your child be able to have a nap someplace quiet during the day? Ask to see every part of the house to which the children have access. Look for guards around fires, safety rails on cookers, doors that small children could lock themselves behind, safety glass on any child height door panels or windows.

Discuss attitudes to discipline. How does she manage difficult behaviour? Clarification on these issues is particularly important. They are common sources of disagreement, even between parents! (Childminders who are members of the National Childminding Association have a policy of not smacking children, even if requested to do so by parents.)

Terms and conditions

Ask what happens when she is ill, or when she takes holidays? Does she have contingency plans with another childminder? If so, ask to see the references of this childminder. (You shouldn't pay for any time off which the childminder takes to suit herself.) What happens when your child is ill, or when you take your holidays, or for hours worked outside the agreed times? What payment will she expect? (Although individual childminders make their own arrangements, it is common practice to pay the normal fee for keeping your place open if your holidays don't coincide. You would not expect to pay for national statutory holidays, unless your child spends them with the childminder: in which case she may charge a higher rate fee. Extra hours may also be liable to a higher rate if outside the childminder's normal working hours, especially if little or no advance notice is given.) Ask whether she uses a formal contract and has written terms and conditions of agreement. Ask if you can have a copy to take home to look at overnight.

References

Ask to see her registration and insurance certificates, references and whether she would mind you speaking to the parents of the other children she minds. If she has nothing to hide she will be only too happy for you to do this. Remember that interviews are two-way! Make sure you give any potential childminder time to ask questions of you.

Taking a business-like approach to choosing child care will help prevent you making a bad choice and reduces the risk of having to start all over again. Do keep the tone friendly though. There's nothing to be gained by making the

My daughter, now 15, still goes back to visit the childminder she had as a baby. They have a very close bond. I think if she was in serious trouble June is the person she would turn to for help. Our two families have become very close.

Nursery school headteacher

childminder feel that she is being interrogated; it gets your relationship off to a bad start. If you can, go to see more than one childminder, and reflect on your visit overnight before coming to a decision. Ultimately your instincts are the best guide of all. Trust them.

My expectations of finding a childminder who would give my daughter the stability of continued care that I wanted for her were quickly shattered. Within two months of having settled her the childminder had to give up work because of a serious illness. For over a month I worked my way through what felt like every childminder in the area, none of them measuring up to my ideals. While I continued my search I worked part of the time at home and took the baby to the office when I had to go in to work. When I at last found my perfect match, I wasn't the only one who heaved a sigh of relief.

Charity sector fundraiser

Pros and cons

Advantages

• Your child will be in a family home environment, with other children.

• Childminders can offer a long-term caring relationship, often taking babies as young as eight weeks and caring for them right through to when they start secondary school.

• Being in a position to set their own hours of work, child-minders have the capacity to be flexible with regard to hours and days of care, and can come up trumps for special occasions, late meetings, unsociable working hours and that inevitable unforeseen emergency.

• She (or he, there are a few male childminders around) may be able to babysit in the evenings: great for your peace of mind if you and your child have already built up a trusting relationship with her.

• Likely to be a parent herself, a childminder will be able to empathise with your needs and worries as a working parent.

• A childminder can be a particularly suitable option for the child with special needs, whether of a medical nature or in order to nurture a particular talent. For instance taking your child for piano/dance/gymnastics lessons.

• Your child has the opportunity to socialise with children of different ages and backgrounds, offering healthy competition and learning experiences which will stand him in good stead when he starts school.

• Living in the local community, childminders are part of the local scene, often having a wide circle of friends and making regular use of facilities in the area such as shops, banks, libraries and children's play centres. This means that your child gets to know, and be known in, his neighbourhood. Chances are good that he will start school surrounded by familiar faces. When you go out with him at

I have come to appreciate the sheer lack of organisation involved in having a childminder. All I have to do is get the children to her and she takes over from there.

Community nurse, mother of two

weekends, you will be able to gauge from comments just how good a choice of childminder you have made.

• Often happy to take children for just part of the week. A good option for part-time workers.

When my wife was rushed into hospital with a suspected brain tumour, Jenny, our childminder, instantly came to my rescue and took Melanie to stay with her throughout Sally's stay in hospital.

Lawyer

Disadvantages

• You will have to deliver your child to the childminder before setting off for work in the morning, and collect him (on time, unless you have made previous arrangements) in the evening.

• You will have no way of being sure just what it is your childminder does with your child during the day.

• You may get little warning if your childminder decides to give up caring for your child.

• You may worry that this paragon of virtue will become a surrogate mother to your child.

• Standards of behaviour between your childminder's family and yours may differ, setting up conflicts and confusion in your child.

• You could experience implied, if not open, criticism about the way you raise your child.

• Tension may be created by resentment from the childminder's own children about the amount of attention she pays to yours.

• You child may be limited to playing in one room. There may be no garden and limited opportunities for playing outdoors as well as for exploring with messy paint, water, sand, playdough etc.

• If the childminder's first language is not the same as yours, your child's ability to communicate may be inhibited and his language development slowed.

• You will have to keep your child away if he has an infectious illness.

Nannies

No longer the domain of royalty and the well-heeled, 'ordinary' families are increasingly opting to employ a nanny. A qualified nanny takes sole charge of the children, including preparing their meals, tidying their rooms, washing their clothes, shopping for them. Sometimes the term is inaccurately used to describe someone who is in effect a mother's help, i.e. someone who has a wider domestic role, less child care responsibility and without formal child care training (see the section School-age Care for more on mothers' helps.) One

Our nanny is terrific. She organises a busy social life for the children and often has hoards of their friends back for tea after school. She has even been known to have a meal ready for us when we come home from work. We couldn't do our jobs without her.

Oil engineer

of the main differences between nannies and childminders is that nannies work in your home and you take on the role of employer. Whether you employ a daily or live-in nanny will depend on your preferences and circumstances. Although it might seem great to have child care on tap, it takes a fair bit of adjustment to get used to sharing your home and child to this degree.

Qualifications

There are a whole range of child care qualifications now on offer, including those issued by the Council for Awards in Children's Care and Education, Norland College (top of the range nannies are trained here), Business and Technical Education Council (BTEC), City and Guilds, National Council for Vocational Qualifications (NVQs), National Association for Maternal and Child Welfare and the Pre-school Learning Alliance. Whatever the qualification remember that primarily they indicate that the holder has completed a course, they don't guarantee the person to be competent, experienced or indeed suitable for work with children. It is for this reason that parents experienced in choosing and selecting child care will often be heard to say that they prefer practical experience and maturity over qualifications. Always ask prospective candidates to let you see their original certificates of qualification, never accept photocopies, and be wary if you are asked to. If you want to know what the nanny had to do to gain the qualification, call up the issuing body.

Finding your nanny

Nannies looking for employment often advertise in specialist magazines such as *The Lady* and *Nursery World*, which are also good sources of information about nanny agencies. Or you could advertise yourself, either in these magazines or through your local press. If you take this route be prepared for the amount of work involved: 'phone calls from and to prospective candidates, and selecting for and arranging interviews. Write your advertisement very carefully so as to screen out unsuitable applicants as much as possible.

Draw up a detailed job description – something that you should do in any case so that you can discuss what the job entails with interviewees, and to form part of the terms and conditions of employment later on. Use it to construct an advert that gives a fair and honest idea of what you are look-ing for, although there is no need to be wordy. Don't bother saying things like 'should be caring and trustworthy', 'needs to like children'. Anyone worth their salt will say they pos-sess these traits in abundance. You can judge for yourself when you interview.

How you want nannies to reply to your advertisement may depend on how much of a hurry you are in to get things sorted. If you have enough time, ask applicants to respond in writing enclosing a CV. Although it will be helpful to give the number and ages of your children, never put their names in an advert – especially one that contains your address and telephone number. Molesters sometimes use these sources to gain access to information about children in their area.

Agencies

Although by far the most expensive way of finding a nanny (fees can be high, as much as the equivalent of two months' salary for your nanny), using a nanny agency can relieve you of a lot of the strain, especially if you are doing it for the first time. The agency will select a number of vetted candidates fitting your detailed requirements for you to select from, having previously checked and verified their references –

although you should always check them yourself too. An agency is also the best way of finding a nanny in an emergency, and to check out local rates of pay.

You'll find agencies for your area listed in your local yellow pages, or by checking out the adverts section of your local papers. Always ask to see agencies' terms and conditions in advance of committing yourself to them. In particular read the small print with regard to refunds in the event of your nanny being unsuitable or not taking up the position or leaving soon after starting. The Federation of Recruitment and Employment Services will supply you with a list of agencies and advise you on agency contracts (see Appendix IV).

Local sources

Speak to other parents to find out what they know about local agencies: they might even be able to recommend a nanny who is looking for work. Local National Childbirth Trust (NCT) groups are a good source of contact with parents who employ nannies. If you spot a nanny in the local park, ask if she is registered with a local agency and what does she think of it? Give yourself plenty of time to find a nanny – up to three months is not unreasonable, though an agency will probably find you one much quicker.

> **Without back-up from a partner I do find it difficult when my son is ill.**
>
> Marketing executive with a multi-national retailing chain

Holding interviews

Start the interview without your child being present if you can, bringing him in towards the end so you can watch how they interact. Give each candidate a copy of the job description together with details of the terms and conditions of employment – see the specimen contract of employment for nannies in Appendix II.

Questions to ask

Ask about experience and most recent posts and whether she is used to being in sole charge? (A nanny whose experience has been gained in a nursery would not be familiar with working in an unsupervised situation.) How many children did she look after? What ages and sex were they? How long was she in each job? Why did she leave? Ask her views about being shared with another family if this is something you might be thinking about (see later) and whether she would mind walking the dog or feeding the cat (she would not automatically see this as part of her job).

Ask about her health (be pragmatic, you can't afford to employ someone who has a recurring illness). Does she smoke? Check out her knowledge of safety in the home (prevention and what to do in case of fires, for instance), first aid, how she would deal with emergencies and stranger danger (such as someone approaching your child while they are out shopping or in the park). Discuss attitudes to discipline. Discuss her creative ideas, both inside and outside the home, and her ability to cook.

Organisational skills and personality

How good is she at organising the day? What social interests does she have? Will she want to have friends to visit? (You will need to make allowances for this eventuality if your nanny lives in or when she is babysitting. Make sure you meet the friends, and ask your children about them.)

For the working parent with unpredictable hours, nothing beats a nanny.

Journalist

117

Note personality and attitude traits. Does she appear:

- lively?
- outgoing?
- confident?
- self-assured?
- helpful?
- interested in you, your work, the children?
- calm?

(You can test most of these if you can prime the baby or children to be a little fractious on interview days!)

Making your choice

When it comes to making your decision trust your instincts and note your children's reactions to the different candidates seriously. Use the interview to ask the reasons for any gaps in employment history, and try to check out responses. Before making your final choice, ensure that everyone in the family meets your prospective nanny, then take 24 hours to think it all over before offering the job – confirming by post once you have taken up her references.

Reference checks

Nannies are not required by law to register with the local authority (unless caring for children from more than two families) and so are not subject to police checks. With this in mind, and because your nanny will be unsupervised while looking after your child, you need to be extremely diligent when choosing a nanny. Don't take references at face value. Speak to referees, preferably face-to-face. People will often tell you more about someone off the record than they are prepared to put down on paper, especially in references they hand to the nanny. Meeting referees will also give you a chance to gauge the values of the family your prospective nanny worked for, giving you a better context in which to place her references.

If you can't visit referees in person write and ask them to send you a written reference in confidence, then discuss it over the 'phone. (As this book went to print the Government was reviewing the terms of the Police Act, under which it had been proposed that employers would be able to ask prospective employees to provide them with a certificate, issued by the Home Office Criminal Records Bureau, listing convictions – if any! The implications were that employers of nannies would have an additional route for checking references. However, at this stage it is unclear whether this will in fact turn out to be the case. Call 0171 217 8226 to check.)

Formalities and legalities

Legally you must provide your nanny with a contract of employment within the first eight weeks of working for you. In fact it makes sense to provide her with one before she starts because this sets out your terms and conditions, which you will want her to abide by from the beginning. And you might have cause to refer to them during the probationary period. The contract states the start date, period of employment and termination notice, salary, hours of employment, holidays, sick pay and sackable offences. You'll find a specimen contract of employment, incorporating all the above points, in Appendix II.

Employment costs

Apart from salary (see the specimen contract in Appendix II), there are other costs associated with a decision to employ a nanny, for instance:

• Your employer's and public liability insurance (your household insurers can provide you with this, which you must have by law).

• Inland Revenue taxes.

• National Insurance Contributions, car insurance and petrol (make sure she is covered by your policy if driving your car, and check the type of insurance cover she has if she uses her own).

• Holiday and sick pay.

• Maternity leave, and pay if she qualifies – remember that nannies have exactly the same employment rights as any other employee.

• Food while on duty.

As an employer, you are responsible for paying her tax and National Insurance Contributions. Call your local Inland Revenue office, tell them you are about to employ a nanny, and ask to be sent an information pack on how to work out tax and National Insurance contributions. Ask to be put through to the Employers' Control Section if you have any problems understanding the paperwork. Alternatively, make an appointment to see a tax inspector at your local tax office who will talk you through the legal procedures.

Nanny share

For a variety of reasons, families sometimes share the same nanny. Approach this option with caution, however, because it may not be in your child's best interests, especially if the nanny is looking after two or more very small children. Will, for example, the ages and sexes of the children make it pos-sible for the nanny to arrange activities that suit all the

The children didn't want to go to their after-school club during the school holidays as well as during term-time. My perfect solution was to share a nanny with a teacher. Her nanny looks after my children during the holidays, when she doesn't need child care.

Office administrator

children? Will she be able to cope with them all safely? Friction can also crop up if there is a mismatch between the two families with regard to values and aspirations. At the risk of labouring the point, looking after small children can be a lonely business, stretching the ability of the most competent of nannies. It would be particularly unwise to expect a young, relatively inexperienced nanny to look after more than one. A nanny looking after a number of very small children will not be able to scoop them up and get out of the house to relieve the tension quite so easily as she could if she was looking after one small baby and an older child, say.

A nanny share can, however, be a very good option if your children are at school and you no longer need full-time care. Getting it right includes being aware of the drawbacks before entering into an agreement, working through them with the other family and taking the nanny's views into account. You will need to agree in whose home most of the caring will be done, how tax and National Insurance will be dealt with, which family will register with the Inland Revenue, and how wear and tear on each other's homes and the cost of heating and electricity will be adjusted for.

Pros and cons

Advantages

• Provides your child with individual attention. In addition, nannies often make friends with other nannies so widening your child's social circle.

• Offers the most flexible type of child care, and for the longest hours, that you are likely to find.

• You can leave your nanny to get your child up and give her breakfast: avoids the stress of trying to get a small child out of the house and still get to work on time.

• You may be able to negotiate some regular babysitting as part of the terms of employment.

• You may be able to reduce your costs by sharing the nanny with another family.

• Your child will be looked after in her own home.

• If an emergency arises at work, it feels more comfortable to ask a nanny to hold on until you can get back than it does to ask a childminder or nursery to care for her until you can get there. Better too for the child as she is already in her own home.

I leave the house at seven every morning, getting home around six thirty. Sarah comes at eight, which is when Sam leaves. There is no other form of child care that would fit my hours.

Medical practitioner

It's a great weight off my mind knowing that if I am held up at work my nanny is flexible enough to wait until I can get back. I also like the fact that my child is safe in her own home and not anxiously waiting for me at the childminder's.

Fashion buyer

• A nanny can fit round the activities of any other children you have in the same way that you would – taking them to after-school activities for instance.

• It means that someone is at home during the day to take in deliveries, let in repair men and deter burglars, etc.

Disadvantages

• Worry about how they are behaving towards your child when you are not around, and

When the parent arrives home at the end of the day can be a very stressful time. Everyone is tired and as sure as eggs are eggs the child who has been as happy as anything throughout the day will burst into tears. The parent thinks he has been miserable all day and you stand there unable to say anything which doesn't sound like an excuse.

A nanny

if they will turn up, are two of the most common anxieties.

• Exploration through messy play with water, sand and paint may be limited – or hard on your furnishings.

• Probably the most costly form of child care, especially as you will be paying her salary from your already taxed pay. Not including tax and National Insurance, the average salary for a daily nanny is in the region of £180 a week (take-home pay). You may also need to provide a car for her, or give her the use of yours, and have the extra expense of heating, food and 'phone bills during the day – though these can be controlled by setting ground rules in advance.

• Nannies don't always stay for very long. This is unsettling for children so try to ensure that the nanny you employ intends to stay for at least a year.

• Not usually interested in part-time work – therefore not a good option if you work part-time.

Now on my fourth nanny I used to fantasise about having one who would stay for many years and become a trusted member of the family. That this hasn't happened seems to have made no difference to the children. Each of our nannies has stayed for a year, each of them brought a different set of strengths and weaknesses. But all of them were very good with the children, who have adapted amazingly well to each change. In fact I'm convinced the comings and goings bother me much more than them.

Barrister

Nurseries

Nurseries come in many shapes and sizes and are registered for business by the local authority on condition they meet a set of standards. The local authority will check that the nursery is based in suitable premises, and meets health, safety, environmental and local planning requirements. It also sets the number and ages of children it can provide places for, checks that it employs the minimum number of qualified staff (including a trained first aider), all of whom have to submit to a police check, and checks that it maintains adequate insurance cover and has written policies about its service. Local authorities will usually try to influence the quality of a nursery's standards, sometimes offering staff access to business and child development training schemes.

Nurseries and learning

Although initially your primary concern may be to find child care that suits your need to continue in, or take up, paid employment it is worth giving some thought to the type of learning philosophy you would like your child to benefit from. To the uninitiated, child care professionals express a bewildering range of views on what is best and appropriate for children of different ages and stages of development. The following is a brief run-down of the main approaches to the early years of learning. At the very least, it will spark questions of your own and help you assess what you want and the quality of a nursery.

Themed approach to learning

Nurseries operating traditional broad-based learning programmes draw on various nursery education philosophies, with an emphasis primarily on suiting individual skills and stages of development – though National Curriculum requirements will also play a part. Structured to a greater or lesser degree by the calibre and experience of the nursery staff, activities will often have a theme about them designed to enhance and extend the child's knowledge and vocabulary. The syllabuses of the Nursery Nurse Examination Board (NNEB) and BTEC place a great deal of emphasis on this approach to learning, so asking about the type of training the nursery staff have should give you a clue to the type of philosophy it operates.

Learning through play

In some nurseries – and particularly in play group settings – learning through play is the primary objective, around which the daily routine is planned. With this philosophy structuring activities or intervening and shaping children's development by asking leading questions is marginal, though here too themes will be used to set the direction of the children's play. Pre-school Learning Alliance certificates as well as courses for play group workers and childminders tend to be biased towards this method.

Didactic methods

Montessori nurseries follow the teachings of Maria Montessori, who developed her teaching methods through her work in the early part of this century – she died in 1952. Montessori methods are somewhat didactic in approach, using specially designed equipment to support activities conducted in a precise manner. For instance, children carry out practical tasks such as pouring or sweeping with real, but scaled-down, household objects. With an emphasis on use of natural materials, Montessori curricula contain large mathematical and language development elements and exclude creative and imaginative activities. A Montessori Teaching Certificate is a must to teach the Montessori curriculum.

Child-centred approach

Introduced from the USA in the middle of the 1980s is a programme of learning called High-Scope, a characteristic of which is the sense of responsibility it seeks to sow in the child for its own actions. For instance, each day has a 'plan, do, review' aspect to its activities. Under this, children, in collaboration with the adults, are encouraged to plan their day, do what they intended to do and review the outcome at the end. There is a High-Scope Institute in the UK which provides training, short courses, advice and information.

Into this category too fall Steiner nurseries and kinder-gartens, which follow the teachings of the Austrian philosopher Rudolph Steiner. Always attached to Steiner schools (of which there are a network of 600 around the world), the approach to learning and development is holistic, with the aim of creating a rounded person at ease with who he or she is. The curriculum is concerned with developing 'all faculties of the human being as a necessary means of support for the modern intellect'. As in Montessori schools, much emphasis is placed on the beauty of the physical environment. At pre-school level the aim is to create an atmosphere akin to a second home, whose element of free-dom is represented in the kindergarten by 'creative play'.

Children start at a Steiner kindergarten at three, gradua-ting to lower school around six and moving to the upper school around fourteen, where they can continue to be edu-cated up to nineteen. Some Steiner centres have play groups and mother and toddler groups attached to them which younger children can attend. Write to Steiner Waldorf Schools Fellowship for further information and a list of where the schools are sited.

Open all hours?

Opening hours vary from nursery to nursery but most open from around 8am to 6.30pm to cater for the needs of working parents, Monday to Friday – although recently a scattering of nurseries have begun to offer 24-hour seven-days-a-week care in response to the needs of shift-workers and family emergencies. The practice of closing for a week to ten days over Christmas and the New Year is common, as well as for all statutory holidays. Although on the increase, places for very young babies are still hard to find.

Finding your nursery

Start with your local authority, which will be able to provide you with a list of registered nurseries in your borough. In addition, your local library is likely to have a printed directory of child care facilities. By their business nature, nurseries advertise their existence widely and often: check your local press and yellow pages.

Making your choice

Start looking and visiting at least three to four months ahead of when you need a place, first, because it is vital that you see as many nurseries in operation as possible so that you can judge the calibre and quality of care available – irrespective of the philosophy involved, which will only ever be as good as the practitioners – and, second, because nursery places tend to be heavily over-subscribed. Over the 'phone check the opening hours, what ages of children they cater for, what the fees are, whether there is a waiting list/vacancy. Ask where it is located exactly and what public transport is near. Ask if it is possible to park by the nursery. Ask to be sent a booklet about the nursery.

Quality checks

When you visit, the following points should be checked:

• Ask about staffing levels, turnover (one of the main criticisms levelled at nurseries is that sometimes staff come and go far too regularly for children to build secure relationships with them) and qualifications.

• Do they employ students?

• Are they supervised?

• Ask about meals, and ask to see where they are cooked and where they are eaten. Is their cost included in the fee?

• Ask how long the nursery has been open, and ask to see its certificates of registration and insurance (these should be prominently displayed on the walls).

• Look at where the children rest during the day.

• Ask what programme of development and learning the nursery follows.

• Does it have policies about equal opportunities, language, race, religion, discipline, poor behaviour?

• How is a typical day structured?

• What procedures are followed when a child is ill, or has an accident on the premises?

• What are fire and safety arrangements like?

• How are children settled in? Are parents invited to play a part in the nursery?

• How is information about the nursery and a child's progress made known to parents?

• Is a deposit required to reserve a place?

During your visit note the 'atmosphere' of the nursery and the attitude of the staff to the children, and their work:

• Are they attentive to the children?

• Are they involved in their activities?

• Do they readily give their attention to a child who asks for it? How is a distressed child being dealt with?

• Are the children enjoying themselves?

• Do there appear to be children sitting alone, or left unattended?

• Is it clean?

When Jenny was pregnant with our second child she was ordered to bed for three weeks. I couldn't possibly have coped without the security of a day nursery. After all, it was unlikely to call in sick!

Computer programmer

• Is it well stocked with toys and play equipment?

• Is the children's work displayed for all to see?

• Were you warmly welcomed?

• Did the children seem pleased to see new faces?

• Is the local culture mix represented, both by the staff and in books, toys, etc.?

• Is there an outside play area that is safe and pleasurable to be in?

I have a very stressful job and found the worry about whether the nanny would let me down at crucial times too much to live with. Although Joe was very happy while she was caring for him, for my peace of mind and so I could concentrate at work, I decided to change to a nursery. It has made a difference to how I am at work. And Joe seems to be just as happy as ever.

Advertising executive

Pros and cons

Advantages

• Carers in group settings provide support for each other, particularly at times when a child is unhappy or going through a difficult phase.

• A good nursery will assign an individual carer to each child for stability and continuity.

• The management structure of nurseries means your child's care will be properly supervised.

• Can offer care from babyhood to school. May even be able to have after-school and holiday care at the same nursery.

• Plenty of opportunities to explore relationships with a range of adults and children, and to develop the social skills of sharing and negotiation.

• Unlikely to close at short notice.

• Not affected by carer sickness – unless everyone is struck down at once!

• Open all year round, except perhaps for bank holidays, Christmas and Easter time.

• Offer sessional care; good if you work part-time.

Disadvantages

• The nursery may not be on your route to work.

• Opening hours may not be flexible enough to meet your needs, especially if you work unpredictable hours.

• You may not like the philosophy of the nursery management, or its philosophy on education.

• Not good for unsociable hours of care – though there is a trickle of nurseries beginning to stay open 24 hours, offering over-night and emergency care.

• You may have to make alternative child care arrangements if your child is ill.

• Great shortage of places for children under two.

• Fees vary a great deal, anything from £90 a week to over £220 a week for full-time care.

I like the fact that Laurence is being looked after by people trained in child development. The nursery is very good about telling me how he is getting on and what he has been doing during the day.

Hospital administrator

Nursery taught Matt a lot about socialising with other children. Now that he is at school I can see the head start going to nursery has given him over the other children. Being used to group social settings he has no problems concentrating even though there is a lot of activity going on around him.

Librarian

Other forms of care

Play groups

Widespread throughout the UK almost every neighbourhood will have a play group in it – usually based in the local community centre or a church hall. Offering a range of care from morning or afternoon sessions to all-day care, termly or all-year round, play groups tend to be for children aged from two to five. Fees are reasonable compared with other forms of care, kept down by the fact that parents are expected to give a fair bit of time to the running of the group. Mainly run by the Pre-school Learning Alliance (PLA), learning through play is the ethos of most play groups. Although they may not fit the needs of working parents, play groups are a good way of meeting other parents. Use the checklists in previous sections to note what you should look for in a good play group, or contact the PLA for information. All play groups should be registered with the Local Authority Social Services.

Because I work part-time I am able to take Lucy two days a week to the local play group. Apart from giving her the chance to make friends with children of her own age, some of whom she will go on to school with, as a single parent it has given me the chance to make friends with people I can socialise with and call on for child care help. In return I babysit for them, which often means taking Lucy with me and putting her to bed with the children I'm looking after.

Clerical assistant

Nursery classes and schools

An important distinction between day care nurseries and nursery classes and schools is of course the fact that the latter are concerned primarily with education in the formal sense, are usually linked to a state primary school, are open term-time only and take children aged three to five. However, private sector nursery schools may take children younger and offer all-day care. For a list of independent schools contact ISIS (Independent Schools Information Service), listed in Appendix IV.

Initially children attend for either morning or afternoon sessions, staying for the whole of the school day – 9am to 3.30pm as a rule – in the term before they enter primary school education at the age of five. Full-time working parents will have to make care arrangements for the end of the day and during school holidays. Evaluate them with the help of the checklists in previous sections. The school or nursery class should be registered with the Education Authority to take three- to five-year-olds, and with Social Services if taking under threes. To find out about state nursery classes and schools, contact the education department of your local authority.

Now our eldest child has started school we are grappling with how to juggle one toddler at a nursery where we work and the other at a school near home. Child care problems never stop, the goal posts keep moving.

Restaurant manager

Babysitting

Although most of us call on family and friends for babysitting, occasionally we ask young people known only casually to us. Whoever we ask, it is probably a fact that this type of care is the one we give the least thought and preparation to. Not a wise move really, perhaps even a little irresponsible. Use the following checklist for guidance:

• Don't ask anyone under sixteen to babysit, especially for babies and toddlers. Apart from the safety angle for your child, if anything happens you will be held legally responsible for the consequences.

• Think about your ideal babysitter qualities and have them in mind when you are thinking of asking someone to babysit. For instance look for someone who is: confident, self-assured, responsible, honest, tolerant, calm, kind, firm, reliable, sensible, shows initiative, etc.

• Encourage a potential babysitter to get to know you and your family well, perhaps by inviting them to tea when your child is around.

• Encourage babysitters to take some first aid training. (It's not a bad idea for parents too. The Red Cross and St John Ambulance Brigade regularly hold first aid sessions at local community centres.)

• Never leave a young babysitter to cope with an already ill child, or to cope alone with several children over a lengthy period of time. (An older and wiser babysitter would probably refuse!)

• Get your feelings about your babysitter having someone to keep them company while they babysit sorted out before you are placed on the spot to give an answer. (You'll have to use your judgement on this one. Don't dismiss it out of hand. Two heads are better than one in some situations.)

• Make sure you leave details for your babysitter of how to contact the emergency services, your doctor and you in a prominent place – in big print by the telephone would be sensible. Check whether they have any knowledge of or training in first aid.

• Familiarise your babysitter with your child's routine and your home. Show her or him where everything is kept, and leave refreshments out for their use.

• Ask neighbours if the babysitter can call on them in an emergency. If the babysitter is young, check that her or his parents know that she or he is babysitting for you.

• Always arrive home at the time you say you will. If you are unexpectedly delayed, telephone your babysitter or get a message through by a neighbour or relative.

• Remember that daytime babysitting carries the extra responsibility of looking after a child who is awake and in need of more supervision.

• Always discuss how the babysitting went. This gives you both a chance to air grievances or worries. Always make safe travel arrangements home for your babysitter, or have her or him stay over.

School-age care

Many mothers return to work when their children reach school age, often assuming that child care is easier for this age group than for the pre-fives. In actual fact, what with the school day ending at 3.30pm and thirteen weeks' vacation times a year, sorting out care for school-age children can be just as challenging. Despite the campaigning efforts of organisations such as the UK national charity Kids' Clubs Network, there are as yet not nearly enough after-school clubs to cater for the needs of all school-age children. However, even *if* every school or neighbourhood had access to an after-school club (the objective of Kids' Clubs Network), your five-year-old might find it too much of a strain to go to a club at the end of the school day, especially in the first couple of terms. Looking at all the options open to you will help you arrive at a decision to suit your child's personality and age.

After-school clubs

Typically open from 3.30pm to 6pm in term-time and all day during the holidays, this type of provision tends to be based in school premises, community centres, village halls or in a purpose-built building. Catering for children aged four to twelve, many clubs will collect children from school and escort them safely to the club. Some also provide preschool breakfast facilities, in which case they will be open from about 7.30am until 9am. During school holidays and on the occasional in-service training days when the school is closed, most clubs are open from 8am until 6pm. All clubs have to be registered with the local authority, which will require them to provide an environment that is stimulating, creative and safe for children, and employ trained staff – whose police records will all be vetted.

Activities and fees

In addition to providing quiet, relaxing areas – even down to some place to sleep – most of the activities on offer will be of the arts and crafts, drama, music, storytelling, games and sports variety. Increasingly, supervision of homework is also undertaken by after-school clubs. Based in schools, community centres and halls, or their own purpose-built premises, clubs are funded or managed in a variety of ways. Attendance fees vary from area to area, with the average being in the region of £15–25 a week for after-school care during term-time, and around £40–50 a week all day during the holidays.

Finding a club

There are a number of ways of locating a kids' or after-school club in your area. Call Kids' Clubs Network for information on clubs in your area (see Appendix IV), ask your local library for a directory of child care facilities registered by your local authority, contact the Under Eights Unit or Registration and Inspection Unit at your Local Authority Social Services Department, ask at local schools, and talk to other parents. Your local Training and Enterprise Council (TEC) may be funding child care facilities, in which case it may well have a child care development officer on its staff; it is worth a call to find out what information she or he can provide you with.

Checking out the quality

Though all clubs catering for children up to the age of eight have to be registered and inspected by the local authority, and meet a certain set of standards, don't assume this guarantees you a quality service. Check out any club you visit using the following as guidance:

• How many children is the club registered for? (The norm is 25–30.)

• What's the ratio of staff to children? (It should be at least one to every eight children.) Ask to see certificates of registration, insurance and quality assurance, for example, that awarded by Kids' Clubs Network.

• How many of the staff are trained? By law at least half the staff should have a relevant qualification or comprehensive experience of working with children. What are salary levels like? These can reflect the quality and experience of staff.

• What qualifications do they hold? (Could include: Playwork or early years' National Vocational Qualifications (NVQs); Nursery Nurse Examination Board (NNEB) Certificate; youth or social work qualifications; teaching or nursing qualifications; Pre-school Learning Alliance Certificate; Kids' Clubs Network Playwork Foundation Certificate or Investing in Playwork Certificate.)

- Ask about the following policies and procedures:
  - opening hours
  - fees
  - admission
  - escorting from school
  - parents being late for collection
  - rules
  - code of behaviour
  - management philosophy
  - health and safety
  - child protection
  - reports on your child while at the club
  - programme of activities
  - policies on discipline and equal opportunities.

- Your child's club record should contain contact names and telephone numbers, information about your child's diet, culture, religion, health, and whether you consent to your child being taken on outings off the premises or for medical treatment in the event of an accident.

- A well-run club with skilled and qualified staff will also encourage you to let the co-ordinator know about school or family issues impacting on your child – bullying, for instance, or if he or she is upset by the absence of a parent – and ask you what you think of the club.

Although Josh's childminder was willing to pick him up from school and keep him until I got back from work, when his primary school opened an after-school club I decided to send him there. Mainly because a number of his friends were going and he wanted to be with them, but also because it's much cheaper than the cost of childminding, it supervises homework, and it is open all during the summer holidays.

Administrator

Holiday camps

In addition to a local kids' club or out-of-school scheme you may have the option of sending your child to a residential holiday camp or daily play scheme during part of the school holidays. The number of companies offering activity holidays for children aged eight to sixteen in the UK and abroad have risen steadily in recent years. With a wide range to choose from it should be possible to find a camp offering the kind of activities your child enjoys. Costs can be high though – anything from £170 to £300 a week! A good travel agent should be able to advise you on an appropriate holiday to suit your child. A directory of over 100 camps can be obtained from The British Activity Holiday Association, whose members abide by a 'quality and safety' code of practice (see Appendix IV).

Play schemes and drop-in centres

Organised by the local authority, voluntary organisations, local employers or private providers, these schemes usually operate during the vacation periods only, especially the summer holidays. Those operated by local authorities tend to be based in schools and community centres and charge a nominal fee, anything from £1 to £5 a day. Privately operated services tend to charge considerably more: £60–170 a week for schemes open from 9am to 5pm each day. The temporary nature of holiday camps, play schemes and drop-ins means they may not be quite so rigorously monitored and inspected as other forms of child care. Use the checklist on page 140 to help you evaluate them.

• Ask about staff qualifications and training. How many years have they been running? What accrediting organisations are they members of?

• Ask about safety records: about illness, accident and emergency procedures. Ask to see its licence to trade, if it has one. (If not ring up the local authority where the facility is based to verify quality and suitability for your child.)

• Ask about: facilities, equipment, activities' programme, accommodation, food, travel to and from the camp or play scheme, the type of clothing needed.

• Ask whether your child will be cared for by the same person throughout his or her stay.

Mother's help

Sometimes described as a nanny, mothers' helps tend not to have formal child care training. Being by implication someone who works with the parent they are often employed by mothers who work from home, both for help with the children and for their wider domestic role (see also 'doula').

When a friend of mine with older teenage children casually mentioned she needed to earn some money but didn't want to 'work' in the formal sense I suggested she become my mother's help. I pay her £260 a month for 20 hours a week. She comes in at 2pm, does some housework before going to pick the children up from school. Depending on the children's social arrangements she will either take them to an after-school activity or bring them home and cook them a meal, often leaving some for me and Sam.

Advertising executive

Usually local mothers themselves, they can be a particularly good solution to the problem of what to do about care for older children during the period when school ends and before the parent gets home (although a mother's help can also be an option for babies and toddlers – something akin to having a childminder come to your own home). The fact that she will also cook the children a meal when she brings them back from school, get them started on their homework, do some washing and ironing is an added bonus.

Finding your mother's help

Notices in local shops are a good way of finding a mother's help; alternatively, ask friends and neighbours. As with every carer, pay particular attention to references. As the people who apply to ads of this nature are likely to live locally, you should find it easier to check out the background and family circumstances of applicants. For reasons mentioned in the section on Nannies, never give the names of your children when advertising for child care help. Unlike a nanny, mothers' helps are deemed to be self-employed so you will not be responsible for their tax and National Insurance. If you offer an attractive rate of pay, say £6 an hour for four hours a day, you are more likely to get good quality candidates applying for the job. Give yourself plenty of time to find one. Start advertising at least six weeks ahead.

Au pairs

The official definition of an au pair is a single person aged 17–27 inclusive who comes to the UK to study English, is treated as a member of the family (which should be English speaking), helps in the home for a maximum of five hours a day, has at least two full days off a week, is given £35–40 a week pocket money and has her or his own room. Although sometimes bracketed with nannies, au pairs are not in the same league at all.

Child care suitability

Mostly in their late teens or early 20s, they are likely to be inexperienced with caring for children, have no child care training, be homesick and in need of parenting themselves! In addition, their command of English may be poor. On top of this, you are unlikely to be able to interview her before she arrives, so neither of you will know if you are going to be able to live with each other until it is too late to change your mind. Although au pairs are, on the whole, not suitable for looking after babies or toddlers, they can be good for someone who just wants help with the housework, or to ward off feeling lonely while at home with a small baby. (Young au pairs should never be expected to take sole responsibility for looking after small babies and children.) Au pairs can, however, be an excellent solution to the question of care for school-age children at the end of the day before parents arrive home from work.

Finding your au pair

On average au pairs tend to stay around for six months. Given their transient nature – this advice applies to nannies also – be cautious about laying out a lot of money before employment. If your au pair comes via informal channels and you pay her expenses to join you, which could be quite a lot if we are talking about air flights, you will have little chance of recuperating these expenses if she ups and leaves within a few weeks. If you go through an agency, check the small print to see if you are guaranteed a replacement au pair, or a refund. The Federation of Recruitment and Employment Services will be able to provide you with a list of agencies whose terms you can check out in advance (see Appendix IV). Send a stamped addressed envelope or international reply coupon.

Other sources are the free Australian and New Zealand papers commonly available outside underground stations in London, the British Association of the Experiment in International Living and the International Catholic Society for Girls (see Appendix IV).

I am currently on my fourth au pair, and though they only stay on average six months at a time, I have found them to be the ideal solution for my children now they are at secondary school. All have been welcome additions to the family. Closer in age to them than me I often find my children engrossed in a serious conversation with the au pair about the merits of the latest music craze. I have one golden rule, however, that I never break. I will not have a teenage au pair!

Doctor

Annual leave

Failing any of the above options being available to you, you may have to be creative with your annual leave. One course of action might be, if your company agrees, to take it all in one go in the summer or for you and your partner to take leave at different times. The latter is obviously not an ideal option because it cuts out family holidays, but it could be a solution in the short term. Whatever arrangements you make for the long summer holidays, don't wait to start sorting them until the vacation period is upon you – places in clubs are snapped up pretty quickly, colleagues may have booked time off when you are wanting it, whilst friends and family who might have been able to help out will have made their own plans by then.

With a husband working overseas, a child who was fed up with the succession of au pairs who came and went like yesterday's news, and a report to write yesterday life was not funny. Something had to give. And my ten-year-old son came up with the solution. He announced he wanted to go to the boarding school where he had visited some friends. I was staggered. It was an option I had never even considered. Particularly as I was an unhappy boarder myself. Three years on I still have a lump in my throat when I take him back on Sunday nights. He, however, loves it!

Senior Civil Servant

....

Crisis management and safety nets

Even the best laid plans can fall apart; child care arrangements are no exception. What's more they have a way of coming apart at the seams just when you need them most! Your nanny 'phones in to say she is too ill to come to work; the nursery has to close because it failed its inspection; your childminder has a family crisis of her own .... Suddenly you have no child care. Experienced working parents usually have some sort of contingency plan to swing into action in an emergency. The following list will either prompt you to dust it off and see if it still works, or help you put one together.

• First port of call: your partner if you have one. The one with the least pressing schedules takes time off. Or takes your child to work.

• Family: if you have some living near you, not at all a foregone conclusion these days, talk to them about whether you can call on their help in an emergency.

• Support networks: seek out and join a local working parents group. Organisations such as the National Childbirth Trust (NCT) and Parents At Work may be able to put you in touch with one. Or look for notices in your local library. Groups of this nature sometimes have lists of members who are able to help out on these occasions.

• Neighbours: get to know them well; there may be a non-working mother among them who might be willing to have your child – in return, say, for babysitting for her.

• Talk over emergency cover with a friend who employs a nanny. As long as we are not talking about touting a sick child around, it may be possible for her nanny to look after your child for a short period of time. Indeed, talk to all your friends about their child care arrangements with a view to calling on them in emergencies. For instance friends' child-minders may be willng to step into the breach in special circumstances.

• Colleagues: discuss with them the possibility of not being able to get into work on the odd occasion and talk about how they could cover for you. To get their co-operation you will need to be able to reciprocate in some fashion.

• Family or compassionate leave: check your company's terms and conditions of employment. You may be surprised to find that they offer a few days' leave a year for situations like the one you now find yourself in.

• Working from home: always a good option to be able to put into action, so be prepared to. Shows your boss you are good at forward planning!

• Employing temporary care: nanny or nursing agencies can help out here – the latter being a better option if your child is ill and you really have no choice but to go into work. Look them up in your yellow pages. Call for details so that you have them to hand, know what they offer, what their fees are, and what accreditation they have long before you need to use one. Investigate the possibility of an insurance savings plan for unforeseen expenditure like this.

• Nursery hotel: some nurseries will take children on a short-term basis and some which style themselves nursery hotels will even keep them overnight. Check out the position of those in your area. In addition to what's been said above about nurseries, ask how they settle a child who is asked to adjust to new surroundings and strange people at short notice.

• Holiday camps, kids' clubs and play schemes, if appropriate: some take children on a daily basis. Be prepared by having details in a file close to hand.

• Call your local authority child care registration department. They may have lists of people or places who look after children in emergencies.

• Take your child to work with you if this is preferable to not being there for a vital meeting or presentation. Get a colleague to take care of him while you attend the meeting or give the presentation – then take him home.

Sudden changes in child care arrangements can be very upsetting for a small child. She may even experience a sense of loss if someone she has come to love suddenly disappears from her life. Try as far as possible to make sure your child knows the person providing cover at short notice, or is familiar with the new environment, e.g. nursery or childminder's home. In the end you may just have to give up all hope of getting to work, no matter how pressing your need is. Use the time constructively by working out what you are going to do about child care for the rest of the week, and sorting out another permanent arrangement, rather than worrying about what is happening at work.

Your relationship with your child's carer

The most common reasons that child care arrangements break down or fall apart is lack of preparation before making a choice, poor co-operation between carer and parents, and lack of mutual trust and respect. Having looked in detail at preparation and selection techniques, this section focuses on the relationship aspect of child care, a crucial element in successful child care arrangements and one on which you can have a major influence.

Childminders and nurseries

Teamwork, trust, respect, diplomacy and an ability to negotiate are vital elements in any relationship, no matter what the circumstances. Sometimes, however, attitudes to roles can lead to awkwardness. Your childminder might adopt a 'grandmotherly' air, offering you advice about how to deal with your child when he is difficult, or maddeningly calming him when you are unable to. Or the nursery might keep you at arm's length or have an air of mystique around their child care methods and practices. Both attitudes can make you feel insecure or a bit of a bystander.

Although you might prickle at the tone adopted by your childminder, don't assume that she is deliberately out to undermine you. It may simply be her way of trying to put you at ease with leaving your child with her. Keep an open mind in any case. Don't shut out what she has to say, her experience is there to be appreciated and valued.

Cultivate good relationships with your child's nursery by showing appreciation for their work in your child's development. Respond to requests for parental involvement, such as joining the management board, helping out at events/ Christmas parties, etc.,

if at all possible. Apart from anything else it's an opportunity to go back stage and really get to know what happens at the nursery when your child is there.

I once became very friendly with the mother of one of the children I minded. Our friendship soured, and eventually ended, because I had to constantly remind her to pay her fees.

Childminder

Nannies

As a result of the nature of the job, sharing care with a nanny presents particular problems. It's a family setting for one thing, though the relationship is one of employer and employee, and it can prove difficult keeping employer/ friend demarcation lines between you and your nanny. The most common cause of breakdown in this form of child care is caused by allowing the job to evolve rather than clearly defining it at the outset, and not respecting each other's roles and privacy. The points listed below may help you avoid some of the pitfalls:

• As soon as your nanny starts give her a list of instructions with regard to sweets, discipline, politeness, table manners, watching television, activities for the children, safety – for example, that she should never leave them outside a shop, or have them round her feet when cooking hot food.

• Discuss your views on socialising with other nannies and the children they care for. Let her know whether you are happy for her to have them come to your home, or for your child to be taken to theirs, how you feel about taking other people's children in the car. Tell her how much money you will leave her for spending on your child during the week – for books or posters or the odd toy, perhaps – and whether you would like receipts – for bookkeeping reasons, not to check on her.

• Give careful thought to boyfriends, friends or relatives visiting while she is working and give her instructions accordingly. Try to introduce her to other carers in your circle of friends to help prevent her feeling isolated – it can be lonely being with a small child all day – as many a parent will know.

• If you have a live-in nanny, state clearly the time you have to be able to get into the bathroom in the mornings – if you share one – when you want to be able to use the kitchen, rules about using the telephone – tying it up with calls to or from friends, how she will pay her share, etc.

• Ask your nanny how she feels about remaining in for plumbers, home deliveries, doing some shopping, etc. Don't simply assume that she will do it.

• Don't call her every five minutes to check that all is well. Encourage her instead to feel free to call you at work if there is a problem.

• Set aside time to discuss progress each week, while at the same time being sure to talk at the beginning and end of each day. This extra time should be during the nanny's normal hours, not additional to. Encourage your nanny to see it as an opportunity for her to tell you about anything that is troubling her.

• Keep her abreast of happenings in your child's life, such as invitations to tea or birthday parties, and whether he needs to bring a present. Likewise, let her know if your child was unwell in her absence.

• Ask her advice, on potty training, for example. Show that you value her experience and expertise.

• Respect the privacy of your live-in nanny, and her need to have friends or relatives visit during the time that she is not working. But by the same token you won't want her social life to impact on you. Being honest and open with each other will help you discuss any annoyances in a friendly manner. Decide how much you are prepared to get involved in her personal life. She may want to keep it private anyway, but just in case it might be wise to keep a certain distance if you don't want to get drawn into love tangles.

• Don't leave the kitchen full of the weekend's washing up and expect your nanny to deal with it on the Monday.

• Leave a note on any food that you are planning to eat when you get back in the evening. Nothing is guaranteed to fray tempers more than coming back to find your supper has been eaten!

• Show your appreciation. Give her a bunch of flowers from time to time. You'll be amply rewarded by the dedication your nanny will show to your child's well-being, if not coming home to the occasional meal!

I draw the line at being faced with the sink piled high with crockery, the rubbish bin overflowing and dirty underwear scattered around the sitting room. Parents forget that their home is actually my workplace.

Nanny

Parting is such sweet sorrow!

Agree with your child's carer how his separation from you will be handled. Nurseries usually have their own rules about this so be guided by them. It's part of the mutual trust that you need to display in order to give your child a positive message that all is well. Equally, experienced nannies and childminders will also be able to suggest how this sometimes quite traumatic event is dealt with. However, be wary if you are advised to simply walk away and leave your child for the whole day at the start of new arrangements. Allow about a week or two for the transition period, when you or your partner will need to be on hand. And never disappear without telling him you are going. This makes your child more clinging and shakes his trust in you. If you can, start settling your child in the last month of your maternity leave. A child who is being cared for in his own home may settle more easily than one who is being cared for in a nursery or childminder's home – where he will have to adjust to strange routines, other children and adults.

Leaving

Have a matter-of-fact attitude about the situation with your child. Don't sound apologetic or give him the idea that he has any choice in the matter. If he senses any hesitation on your part he'll play to it. Talk about the changes in an upbeat way, making them sound interesting and exciting for him. If you are using a nursery or childminder, it's fairly common to start your child off by leaving him for a couple of hours or a morning. If he is old enough to understand the concept of time, tell him when you will be back. Lengthen the time you leave him until eventually you reach the full amount of hours you need. Sometimes, no matter what you do your child determines to make you squirm by crying miserably each time you attempt to leave.

Leaving my son at nursery for the first time was dreadful. Clinging to my knees and crying as though his heart was breaking, he had to be pried from me. In floods of tears myself by this time and in no fit state to face the public I sat down just outside the nursery door ... and couldn't believe my ears when, a few minutes after I had left this supposedly distraught child, I heard him laughing.

Estate agent

Professional judgement

Good nurseries and experienced childminders and nannies will help you judge when it is best to leave. Obviously no-one likes to walk away from a child who is upset, but if all efforts to prevent this fail it is often best to give her a warm and bright hug and leave the carer to distract her and take the focus off your departure. This method is usually easiest on all concerned. Call your nanny, childminder or the nursery later to find out how things are. Chances are that she will have stopped crying and started to explore her new surroundings a few minutes after your departure. If your child continues to be upset despite a reasonable settling-in period, probe more deeply to find out why. It is also important to be prepared to change to another nursery if she continues to be unhappy.

Finally, don't underestimate the amount of stress and tension you will feel while you and your child adjust to separation. Line some treats up for yourself during this time to take your mind off how she is getting on, or watching the clock until it is time to go and collect her. Your anxiety will show you know, and it will only serve to keep the agony going for longer. Go swimming or have your hair done.

What your child's carer needs to know

Age, temperament and whether your child is used to being cared for by others will all play a part in how easily she settles. Giving the nursery, nanny or childminder a comprehensive picture of your child will help keep stress to a minimum. Tell them about:

• Her sleep patterns, the routine she is used to, the type of food she likes, any special dietary needs, how you make up her milk bottles, whether she is allowed sweets and any medical issues they should know about, such as allergies, medicines that she is currently taking, etc.

• The sort of games she likes to play, whether she prefers quiet activities, or rushing about, whether she enjoys being read to or looking at books herself, her favourite toy – best left at home if she is being cared for outside her home as she may be further upset by having to share it with the other children – and whether she uses a comfort blanket – which she should bring with her if she is going to a nursery or childminder.

• Keep them informed of any changes at home that might add to her distress, etc. Always give your carer important telephone numbers, such as you and your partner's work numbers, that of your doctor and your older child's school – to warn them of an emergency that might prevent her being picked up on time at the end of the day, for instance.

Making sure all is well

Parents often worry whether they will be able to tell if their child is unhappy with a carer. You will know when something is wrong, even if you only have the faintest unease that something is amiss, your antennae will be up: don't ignore your instincts. Your child's behaviour is the best monitor you have; note any changes, no matter what their age. Some of the signs that will warn you all is not well with a young child include:

• Not wanting to let go of your hand.

• Seeming fearful when in the presence of the carer, or about going to school.

• Reverting to wetting his pants.

• Clinging to you with frightening desperation when you leave him, or showing great anxiety to be taken home as soon as you arrive.

• Always tearful or withdrawn when you collect him from the nursery or childminder, or take over from your nanny.

The chances are that your child will have shown some advance signs that something was wrong long before getting to this stage.

I knew I was going to have to make other arrangements when my two-year-old swore at me one night!

Book designer

It pays to talk

Chatting to her about her time with her carer will help you nip any problems before they get to crisis proportions. Always listen carefully to her fears and concerns and encourage her to feel free to tell you if she is ever worried about anything – no matter what age your child is. Don't wait until you suspect a problem. Involving yourself in the nursery, going on an outing with your childminder or your child's school class, arriving home unexpectedly, giving local shopkeepers and neighbours opportunities to talk about how your child and carer are together are some examples of how you might monitor her care without seeming to. But before you go leaping to any assumptions about the quality of her care reflect on whether *you* are giving off vibes that could be unsettling her:

• Are you and your partner arguing more of late?

• Are you under stress at work? Are you paying less attention to her?

• What's your relationship with her carer like?

• Do you show respect for each other?

• Disagree with each other fundamentally?

Any one of these factors could affect your child's behaviour. If you feel able to, give the nanny/childminder/nursery a chance to tell you why they think your child is unhappy, and what they propose to do about it. Talking to other parents whose children are being cared for by your childminder, or attending the same nursery, could either confirm your suspicions or reassure you that your child hasn't been harmed in any way. If you can't quell your fears that something is wrong, end the arrangement immediately.

I instantly dismissed my nanny when my neighbour told me she was smacking my child.

Train driver

CHAPTER 7

Survive and thrive

Each of us leads a different lifestyle, and we each have different strengths, weaknesses, wants and needs. Each of us discovers our own ways of surviving and enjoying working parenthood. These are some of the ways other parents survive and balance their working lives with family life. They are offered to comfort, enlighten and amuse you. Happy working parenthood!

I have everything I can delivered.

We shop – children in tow – in bulk once a month, choosing the quietest time at the supermarket and letting assistants at the store do the packing.

I treat myself once a week to a good take-away.

My husband looks after our children full-time so I am able to go swimming every night after work.

I have a shiatsu massage once a month.

We give each other a 'free' weekend once a month. Which means that for a whole weekend you are not responsible for any part of running the house or taking care of the children. My partner tends to do some DIY on his free weekend. I like to have a day out with friends who don't have children, but mostly I just get up late and lounge around.

No matter how tight the finances, I have a sauna once every two weeks. It seems to clear my mind as well as my pores!

I work out in a gym once a week, helps keep me fit and get rid of pent up frustrations.

Children in tow, I go for a very long walk in the park every weekend. It gets us out of the house and puts us in a better mood with each other. We often play some kind of board game when we come home.

Every so often my partner and I have a bloody good row. It works wonders for our sex life!

We send the children to their grandparents for a long weekend about every six months, then we book into a hotel for a heavy petting session!

My husband leaves the house at 6am and rarely gets home before 10pm. With such long hours I didn't feel I could cope with full-time work so I returned part-time. I also employed a cleaner and a gardener.

Every week I have to commute between Edinburgh, where my home is, and London, where I work. Having one complete set of underwear, socks and shaving gear in each place means I never have to worry about making sure I have packed them – or carry their weight.

We sent the dog to board with my parents. I was feeling guilty that I couldn't give him as much of my attention with a new baby in the house. I also couldn't bear the thought of walking him every day!

I decide what level of chaos I can live with and don't worry about the rest.

I never iron if I can help it. I hang the washing up so that it drip dries. If I have to iron, I do it sitting down and watching television.

There's nothing like kneading dough for working off stress. At least we never run out of bread!

Among my friends I'm regarded as something of an oddity. I actually like housework! It's boring, it's dull and it is also amazingly relaxing and therapeutic. I find it a great way to unwind.

We couldn't survive without our diaries. My partner and I meticulously write down everything we are doing, and have a 'diary meeting' once a week to check when we are going to be together and which of us is going to do what with the children.

I keep back some leave for taking the occasional half day off during the long summer holidays to spend time with my teenage children – prevents me from feeling guilty or frustrated at missing out on being with them.

I've discovered that the best way to find out how my son is feeling about himself is to do something with him that he enjoys – like playing football. He clams up if I ask direct questions at other times.

I have three teenage sons and was in danger of losing touch with them. So I make sure I take each of them out for a day on their own during the school holidays. This one-to-one time has become very precious to all of us. As a family we also always eat together in the evenings.

I felt really bad about the way my first child had a succession of childminders so I wasn't looking forward to my second child having the same experience. My mother came to the rescue. She decided to take early retirement so she could raise my son. He spends week days with her and weekends with me and his sister.

As the youngest of six I watched my mother get progressively more despondent about her 'role' in life as each child left the nest. I realised that she lived her life through and for each of her children. The experience made me resolve never to do this to my own children. I lead a very full and active social life which is separate from my family life, and which frees my children from feeling any guilt about spending time with their old dad!

I gave up feeling guilty. There was no point. I couldn't be Superwoman so I settled for who I was.

Appendices

Appendix I:
Child care good practice

As a final note on what to look for when assessing nurseries and childminders, the 1989 Children Act set out guidelines to help local authorities assess the quality of care on offer. They offer useful guidance for any child care setting.

• Programmes should be planned before the children arrive for the day.

• Activities should be appropriate to the child's age and level of development.

• Young children should have learning opportunities, including a wide range of toys. Visits and outings should be arranged for school-age children, whilst equipment and facilities on offer should allow for art and craft, sport and games, drama, music and constructive activities.

• Activities should be planned with the children.

• Areas should be set aside for both quiet and noisy activities.

• Children should be allowed to work at their own pace.

• Policies on behaviour and discipline should be appropriate to the age of the child, and agreed with the parent.

• Adults should respect the dignity and individuality of the children in their care, and respond to them with affection and sensitivity.

• Parents should be kept fully informed about their child's activities and progress.

• Clear arrangements for emergencies should always be in operation, and agreed with parents.

• A first aid box should always be on hand, and preferably also a member of staff trained in first aid.

Appendix II:
Contract of employment

Most parents who employ a nanny find they never have cause to refer to terms and conditions of employment or job descriptions after the initial discussion about what is involved and expected. However, it is better to err on the side of caution and give your nanny a formal contract together with a full job description, just in case.... Intended for guidance only the following covers the minimum legal requirements of a contract of employment. Use the section on Nannies in Chapter 6 to help you draw up a job description.

1 Name and address of employer.

2 Name and address of employee.

3 Job title, e.g. Daily nanny/Live-in nanny.

4 Date (employment is to start).

5 Salary: state how much it is before tax and National Insurance (NI) deductions, whether it will be paid in cash or by cheque, when (which day of the week or month), and that NI Contributions will not be contracted out of SERPS – unless there is a company pension scheme in operation, which is unlikely in the circumstances. Social Security employer's advice line – 0345 143 143 – will advise you on this.

State also the date on which her salary will be eligible for review, usually once a year, and the hourly rate she will be paid for any extra hours worked – such as for babysitting if she is willing. (The UK weekly average for a daily nanny is around £180 net, a total cost to you of over £260 a week when you add in employee and employer tax and NI Contributions.)

6 Probationary period: say how long this will be for – usually a four-week period.

7 Hours of work: state what her normal start and finish times will be and the maximum number of hours she will be expected to work, allowing for unforeseen events (8am to 7pm is fairly typical – but don't stretch her goodwill by expecting too much or being home too late, as this is the fastest way to lose a nanny). Bear in mind here that recent legislation could make it illegal for employers to expect employees to work longer than 48 hours a week. However, if the employee agrees to the hours there is no problem. (Check where you stand with ACAS or the TUC.)

In the case of a live-in nanny state what days she will be off during the week and/or how many weekends/days a month. (The norm tends to be alternate weekends off plus two extra days – a total of six days off a month.)

8 Holidays: state how many weeks' paid leave she will be entitled to, and that they must be arranged with your agreement.

9 Sickness: all you need say here is that Government legislation will apply. Call Social Security advice line 0345 143 143 for information on Sick Pay.

10 Maternity pay and leave: nannies have the same rights as all other employees. Unless you intend otherwise state that current legislation will apply.

11 Insurance: you should state that you are insured against claims for injuries – Employer and Public Liability Insurance. Contact your household insurers for clarification.

12 Termination of contract: state how this will happen, i.e. by each giving x weeks' notice in the first year and x weeks in the second, etc. By law an employee is entitled to one week's notice in the first two years or less of employment and to one week's notice for each year of service after that – up to a maximum of 12. An employer is entitled to one week's notice irrespective of length of service unless otherwise stipulated in the contract.

13 Pensions: state that you do not operate a pension scheme.

14 Grievances: contact ACAS (Advisory, Conciliation and Arbitration Service) for advice. Like any other employee, a nanny can sue for wrongful or constructive dismissal, so it would be wise to make sure that you have some sort of procedure in place for dealing with serious grievances – on both sides.

15 Sackable offences: list what would give you cause for such action, for example, stealing, lying, drug taking, neglecting or being cruel to the children (such as smacking them), being persistently unreliable, gross incompetence, having boyfriends in the house, false references, gossiping about your family, etc.

16 Signed and dated by employer.

17 Signed and dated by employee.

Give your nanny one copy of the contract and keep one for yourself.

Appendix III:
Statutory parental leave
in other countries

AUSTRIA
Maternity leave: 16 weeks at 100 per cent salary.
Right to return: Yes, if returning after 16 weeks.
Paternity leave: None by right.

Parental leave: Unpaid parental leave up to child's second birthday, or fourth if taken part-time. Right to return to work protected, though not to the same job.
Special/Family/Emergency leave: One week's paid leave a year to care for close family.

BELGIUM
Maternity leave: 5 weeks at between 75 per cent and 81 per cent of gross salary.
Right to return: Either parent has the right to return part-time if they wish.
Paternity leave: 3 days on full salary.
Parental leave: At least 12 weeks' unpaid leave, up to a maximum of 52, with job protection. Can be taken by either parent and tagged onto maternity leave.
Special/Family/Emergency leave: Employees who have been with the same employer for one year may take a career break of between 6 and 12 months. Up to 2 days' paid leave is available for domestic emergencies, and 10 days' unpaid leave by employer agreement.

DENMARK
Maternity leave: 18 weeks on 90 per cent of salary.
Right to return: Yes.
Paternity leave: 10 days' paid leave.
Parental leave: 10 weeks' paid parental leave available for either parent following maternity leave with job protection.
Special/Family/Emergency leave: Unpaid statutory leave of 3 months plus a further 9 months under employer/union collective agreement. Possible to take sabbatical leave of up to a year.

FINLAND
Maternity leave: 17.5 weeks on 66 per cent of salary.
Right to return: Yes, and to work part-time if the child is under school age.
Paternity leave: One week's paid leave.

Parental leave: 163 working days to either parent following maternity leave on 66 per cent of salary with the right to re-instatement.

Special/Family/Emergency leave: Employees can take child care leave up to a child's third birthday, unpaid once maternity and parental leave have been used up. In addition, 4 days' sick leave a year may be taken to care for children under 10.

FRANCE

Maternity leave: 16 weeks on 84 per cent of salary.

Right to return: Yes, if the parent returns before the child's first birthday – *see also* Parental leave.

Paternity leave: 3 days' paid leave.

Parental leave: Either parent can take full-time or part-time unpaid parental leave until the child is three.

Special/Family/Emergency leave: 1–4 days' unpaid leave depending on circumstances.

GERMANY

Maternity leave: 14 weeks on sick pay rate. May be topped up by employer.

Right to return: Yes – *see also* Parental leave.

Paternity leave: None by right.

Parental leave: Either parent may take unpaid parental leave until the child reaches 36 months, with job protection.

Special/Family/Emergency leave: Some employees entitled to 10 days' leave to care for a sick child.

GREECE

Maternity leave: 18 weeks on full salary.

Right to return: Yes – *see also* Parental leave.

Paternity leave: 2 days, paid.

Parental leave: Either parent may take unpaid leave until child reaches two and a half. Right to job back or similar.

Special/Family/Emergency leave: Up to 10 days' unpaid leave a year to care for a sick child or spouse. In addition up to 4 days per year for school progress reports.

IRISH REPUBLIC

Maternity leave: 14 weeks on 70 per cent of salary.

Right to return: Yes.

Paternity leave: None by right.

Parental leave: None by right as yet. Expected June 1998.

Special/Family/Emergency leave: None by right; however, Civil Servants are allowed up to 6 months' unpaid leave for domestic reasons or up to 2 months to care for a sick relative. Employer/union collective agreements grant other employees up to 3 days' leave for family reasons.

ITALY

Maternity leave: 20 weeks on 80 per cent of salary.

Right to return: Yes – *see also* Parental leave.

Paternity leave: None by right.

Parental leave: Either parent may take leave for 6 months before the child's first birthday with the right to return to the same job.

Special/Family/Emergency leave: Employer/union collective agreements grant employees up to 30 days' leave on marriage and up to 2 days a year for family reasons.

LUXEMBOURG

Maternity leave: 16 weeks on full salary.

Right to return: Yes, if returning after maternity leave – *see also* Parental leave.

Paternity leave: None by right.

Parental leave: None by right. However, public sector workers can take up to one year of unpaid leave for either parent following maternity leave. In addition they have the right to return on a part-time basis until the child starts school, and at any time up to a child's fifteenth birthday. Private sector workers who take a year off following the birth of a baby may apply for re-engagement. Legislation expected June 1998.

Special/Family/Emergency leave: None by right.

THE NETHERLANDS

Maternity leave: 16 weeks on full salary.

Right to return: Yes – *see also* Parental leave.

Paternity leave: Up to 3 days, paid.

Parental leave: Either parent may take up to 6 months' unpaid part-time leave until a child reaches four. In the case of Civil Servants this leave is paid.

Special/Family/Emergency leave: Employer/union collective agreements grant employees up to 4 days' leave a year for family reasons.

NEW ZEALAND

With the exception of special leave all forms of leave are unpaid. To qualify an employee must have worked at least 10 hours a week for the same employer for 12 months leading up to the expected date of confinement. During pregnancy mothers are allowed up to 10 days' leave for antenatal care.

Maternity leave: 14 weeks – or a period agreed by the employer if adopting a child under five.

Right to return: The employer is required to keep the employee's job open for four weeks only; after this he can decide that the post is a key position and cannot be filled by a temporary replacement.

Paternity leave: Up to 2 weeks, both for the birth of a natural child and in the case of adoption.

Parental leave: Up to 12 months, to be taken before the child's first birthday or anniversary of an adopted child. Parental leave can be taken by either parent or shared between them, although any period taken as maternity leave is deducted from the total available. Paternity leave is additional to the 12 months.

Special leave: After completion of 6 months' employment with the same employer, employees are entitled to 5 days' paid special leave which can be taken if: the employee is ill; the spouse is ill; a dependent child or parent of the employee is ill; or on the death of the employee's spouse, child, parent, brother, sister, grandparent, father-in-law or mother-in-law.

PORTUGAL
Maternity leave: 98 days on full salary.

Right to return: Yes; also the right to return on a part-time or on a flexible hours basis for a period of 6 months to 3 years until the child reaches 12, depending on employer agreement. *See also* Parental leave.

Paternity leave: None by right.

Parental leave: Either parent may take unpaid leave of between 6 and 12 months following maternity leave with the right to reinstatement.

Special/Family/Emergency leave: Employees are allowed up to 30 days a year of paid leave to care for a sick child under 10 and up to 15 days a year unpaid leave to care for a sick relative, including children under 10.

SPAIN
Maternity leave: 16 weeks on 75 per cent of salary.

Right to return: Yes – *see also* Parental leave.

Paternity leave: 2 days' paid leave.

Parental leave: Either parent may take up to three years' unpaid leave but has the right to job reinstatement in the first year only. In addition either parent can opt to work part-time until the child is 6 years old.

Special/Family/Emergency leave: Career breaks of between 2 and 5 years are allowed for family reasons, but without the guarantee of job reinstatement. Up to 4 days' paid leave a year is allowed to care for a sick child.

SWEDEN
Maternity leave: 12 weeks on 90 per cent of salary.

Right to return: Yes – *see also* Parental leave.

Paternity leave: 10 working days allowed on 80 per cent of salary.

Parental leave: Either parent may take full-time parental leave until a child is one and a half or return part-time until a child is eight. Of this leave 360 days are paid at 80–90 per cent of salary. Employees have the right to reinstatement or to a similar job.

Special/Family/Emergency leave: Either parent is allowed 60 days per year per child for care reasons on 80–90 per cent of salary, and 2 days' leave on full pay is allowed for school visits.

UNITED KINGDOM
Maternity leave: 14–40 weeks, depending on employment service. First 6 weeks on 90 per cent of average salary then 12 weeks on sick pay rate.
Right to return: Yes: at the end of 14 weeks for all employees, at the end of 40 weeks for employees who have 2 years' continuous employment.
Paternity leave: None by right.
Parental leave: None by right.
Special/Family/Emergency leave: None by right.

UNITED STATES OF AMERICA
Under the Family and Medical Leave Act (FMLA) 1993, eligible employees are entitled to take up to 12 weeks of unpaid, job-protected leave for family or medical reasons in a 12-month period specified by the employer. The Act applies to employees of public (government) agencies and private sector employers who employed 50 or more employees in 20 or more work weeks in the current or preceding calendar year. To be eligible for FMLA benefits, an employee must have worked for the same employer for a total of 12 months, have worked at least 1,250 hours over the previous 12 months, and work at a location where at least 50 employees are employed by the same employer within 75 miles.
Leave entitlement: A covered employer must grant an eligible employee up to a total of 12 weeks' unpaid leave during a 12-month period for one or more of the following:
• Birth and care of the employee's newborn child.
• Adoption or foster care of a child.
• To care for an immediate family member with a serious health condition.
• Or if the employee is unable to work as a result of her or his own medical condition.

Spouses employed by the same employer are jointly entitled to a combined total of 12 weeks' leave. In some circumstances an employee may be able to extend their leave by reducing the hours that they normally work.

·······················

Appendix IV: Useful organisations

ACAS (Advisory, Conciliation and Arbitration Service)
0171 396 5100 (advice line)
For advice on employment contracts, rights and grievances.

Association of Breastfeeding Mothers
Sydenham Green Health Centre, 26 Holmshaw Close, London SE26 4TH
0181 778 4769
Aims to promote and support breast-feeding. Runs support group meetings throughout the UK and operates a telephone counselling service.

Association for Postnatal Illness
25 Jerdan Place, London SW6 1BE
0171 386 0868
Advises and supports women suffering from postnatal depression. Operates a network of support volunteers throughout the UK.

The Benefits Agency
RPFA Unit (Correspondence), Room 37D, DSS Longbenton, Benton Park Road, Newcastle upon Tyne NE98 1YX
For Retirement Pension forecast.

The Benefits Agency, Pensions and Overseas Benefits Directorate
DSS, Tyneview Park, Whitley Road, Benton, Newcastle upon Tyne NE98 1BA
For information on Social Security rights when moving to another country.

The British Activity Holiday Association
Orchard Cottage, 22 Green Lane, Hersham,
Walton-on-Thames, Surrey KT12 5HD
01932 252994 (9am–1pm)
Monitors standards of safety and quality of instruction. Acts as professional association for members. Publishes a directory of UK holiday camps and activity centres of BAHA members.

British Association of the Experiment in International Living (EIL)
01684 562577
Set up in 1936 it aims to promote understanding, friendship and respect between people from different cultural backgrounds. Arranges homestays in the UK for foreign nationals, international homestay programmes and an au pair scheme to the USA.

British Red Cross Society
9 Grosvenor Crescent, London SW1X 7EJ
0171 235 5454
For information on local First Aid courses.

Business and Technical Education Council (BTEC)
Central House, Upper Woburn Place, London WC1H 0HH
0171 413 8400
For an explanation of curriculum content of child care BTEC training courses.

Campaign Against Bullying At Work (CABAW)
Mulberry Cottage, Fordy Lane, East Hendred,
Oxfordshire OX12 8JU
01235 834548
Launched at the House of Lords in 1996. Operates support and advice helplines for people being harassed at work.

Centre for Economic Policy Research
25–28 Old Burlington Street, London W1X 1LB
0171 878 2900
Independent think-tank. Possible source of statistical material for making a business case against unfriendly working practices.

Childcare Solutions
50 Vauxhall Bridge Road, London SW1V 2RS
0171 834 6666
A nationwide search and find child care information service, bought on subscription by employers for use by their employees. Also the source of Childcare Vouchers, provided to employees as an employment benefit by employers.

Child Poverty Action Group
4th floor, 1–5 Bath Street, London EC1V 9PY
0171 253 3406
Strong on benefit rights. Good source of information on Childcare Disregard.

Child Support Agency
Headquarters, 24th Floor, Millbank Tower, 21–24 Millbank, London SW1 4QU
0345 133133 – for enquiries.

Children's Legal Centre
University of Essex, Wivenhoe Park, Colchester, Essex CO4 3SQ
01206 873820
Represents the interests of children and young people with regard to the law and policy relating to them. Operates a free advice and information service by 'phone and letter.

Choices In Childcare
14–18 West Bar Green, Sheffield S1 2DA
0114 276 6881
Publishes directory of children's day care and education information services throughout the UK.

Citizens First
0800 581 591
For free factsheets on working and living in a European Union member state, including: National Education Systems, Right to Stand as a Candidate in European Parliament Elections and Right of Residence.

City and Guilds
1 Giltspur Street, London EC1A 2DD
0171 294 2468
For information on vocational courses and content, including child care.

City Women's Network
PO Box 353, Uxbridge, Middlesex UB10 0UN
01895 272178
Business, professional and social network for senior executive women. Organises a range of events, including Take Our Daughters to Work Day (April).

COFACE (Confederation of Family Organisations in the European Community)
17 rue de Londres, B-1050 Brussels, Belgium
+32 (2) 511 41 79

Contact a Family
170 Tottenham Court Road, London W1P 0HA
0171 383 3555
Promotes mutual support between families caring for children with any type of disabilities or special need. Helps establish local support groups throughout UK.

Council for Awards in Children's Care and Education
8 Chequer Street, St Albans, Hertfordshire AL1 3XZ
01727 847636/967333
Offers specialised training in children's care and education. An awarding body for NVQs and NNEB Diplomas in Nursery Nursing.

CRY-SIS Support Group
BM CRY-SIS, London WC1N 3XX
0171 404 5011 (daily 8am–11pm)
Provides practical advice to parents of babies who cry incessantly and have sleep problems. Also older children with temper tantrums, clinging and long-term crying difficulties.

Day Care Trust
4 Wild Court, London WC2B 4AU
0171 405 5617
Provides information about child care costs and availability, as well as campaigning for better provision. Operates an information helpline.

Department for Education and Employment
Sanctuary Buildings, Great Smith Street, London SW1P 3BT
0171 925 5000
Library 0171 925 5189
For information on statutory employment rights.

Employers For Childcare
Fiona Cannon, Chair, Westminster Communications,
Cowley House, Little Cottage Street, London SW1P 3XS
0171 976 7374
A consortium of over 15 major businesses promoting the benefits of family friendly practices among employers.

Employment Service Overseas Placing Unit
Rockingham House, 123 West Street, Sheffield S1 4ER
0114 259 6086/6089
For advice on working abroad and information on job vacancies in other EU member states (EURES).

EPOCH (End Physical Punishment of Children)
77 Holloway Road, London N7 8JZ
0171 700 0627
Provides positive advice for parents and other carers.

Equal Opportunities Commission
Work and Family Unit, Overseas House Quay Street,
Manchester M3 3HN
0161 833 9244
Will advise on whether or not there are grounds for action in cases where a parent either loses a job or experiences harassment because of family commitments.

Exploring Parenthood
4 Ivory Place, Treadgold Street, London W11 4PB
0171 221 6681 (advice line)
Aims to prevent stress and breakdown in family life by offering a one-stop support service which any parent can use.

Faircheck Limited
Claremont House, 22 Claremont Road, Surbiton,
Surrey KT6 4QU
0181 390 0999
Provides a vetting service designed specifically to assess the suitability of people seeking child care work.

Families Need Fathers
134 Curtain Road, London EC2A 3AR
0181 886 0970 (information line)
Concerned primarily with maintaining a child's relationship with both parents following separation and divorce.

Fawcett Society
45 Beech Street, London EC2Y 8AD
0171 628 4441
Founded in 1866 from the Suffragist movement, the Society campaigns on employment, financial security and the sharing of domestic responsibility, with the aim of achieving economic and social independence for women.

Federation of Recruitment and Employment Services (FRES)
36–38 Mortimer Street, London W1N 7RB
0171 323 4300
Members of FRES sign up to a code of practice. Can supply a list of member nanny and au pair agencies.

Gingerbread
16–17 Clerkenwell Close, London EC1R 0AA
0171 336 8184 (advice line)
Provides day-to-day support and practical help for single parents and their children through a UK-wide network of self-help groups. Excellent source of information on benefit rights.

Gingerbread Ireland

12 Wicklow Street, Dublin 2

+353 (1) 710291

Serves same function as Gingerbread in the UK.

HAPA – Adventure Play for Children with Disabilities and Special Needs

Fulham Palace, Bishop's Avenue, London SW6 6EA

0171 736 4443/0171 731 1435

Offers a national information service on all aspects of play and disability. Organises holiday playschemes, Saturday and after-school clubs.

High-Scope Institute

Copperfield House, 190–192 Maple Road, London SE20 8HT

0181 676 0220

For information on the High-Scope method and philosophy of early years' education.

Home-Run

Cribau Mill, Llanvair Discoed, Chepstow, Gwent NP6 6RD

01291 641 222

A networking and advice-style newsletter for the self-employed.

Home-Start UK

2 Salisbury Road, Leicester LE1 7QR

0116 233 9955

Offers regular support, friendship and practical advice to families who are experiencing difficulties and stress. Trained volunteers, who are normally parents, visit families in their homes, helping to prevent family crisis and breakdown. There are 140 schemes throughout the UK and some overseas.

Hyperactive Children's Support Group

71 Whyke Lane, Chichester, West Sussex PO19 2LD

01903 725182

Offers support, information and practical ideas to parents of hyperactive children.

IFA (Independent Financial Advisers) Promotion
0117 971 1177
For a list of independent financial advisers in your area.

Incomes Data Services (IDS)
77 Bastwick Street, London EC1V 3TT
0171 250 3434
IDS is an independent research organisation providing information on pay, employment conditions, pensions and labour law.

Industrial Relations Services
18–20 Highbury Place, London N5 1QP
0171 354 5858
Monitors employment legislation and equal opportunities in the workplace. Conducts frequent surveys of corporate family friendly policies.

Industrial Society
Robert Hyde House, 48 Bryanston Square, London W1H 7LN
0171 262 2401
An independent advisory and training body. A useful source of information on good employment practices.

Institute of Personnel & Development (IPD)
IPD House, 35 Camp Road, London SW19 4UX
0181 971 9000
For information and research reports on employment conditions.

International Catholic Society for Girls
St Patrick's International Centre, 24 Great Chapel Street,
London W1V 3AF
0171 734 2156 (Tues, Thurs 11am–3pm; Sun 2–5pm)
Provides a placement service for au pairs in the UK and abroad. Also a social network for au pairs themselves.

ISIS (Independent Schools Information Service)
3 Vandon Street, London SW1
0171 222 7274
For lists of independent schools and prep schools.

Kiddicare Association
Dennis House, Hawley Road, Hinckley, Leicestershire LE1 0PR
01455 233252
Represents the interests and views of members to authorities,
public bodies and ministers, with the aim of maintaining high
standards in private nurseries. May be able to provide parents
with a list of members, or details of a local nursery.

KIDS
80 Waynflete Square, London W10 6UD
0181 969 2817
Provides a range of local services to parents aimed at enabling
children with special needs to be children first and to fulfil their
hopes and aspirations.

Kids' Clubs Network
Bellerive House, 3 Muirfield Crescent, London E14 9SZ
0171 512 2112/0171 512 2100 (information line)
Working towards a kids' club in every neighbourhood, urban and
rural. Offers a range of information and advice to parents, schools
and employers on how to set up a club or locate one locally. Can
also provide details of Training and Enterprise Councils with a
child care development officer on staff.

La Leche League of Great Britain
Box BM 3424, London WC1N 3XX
0171 242 1278
Provides personal help, information and support to mothers wish-
ing to breast-feed.

LECs (Local Enterprise Companies)
Customer Service Desk, Scottish Enterprise,
120 Bothwell Street, Glasgow G2 7JP
0141 248 2700
Highlands and Islands Enterprise,
Bridge House, 20 Bridge Street, Inverness IV1 1QR
01463 234171
For lists of LECs in Scotland.
See also Kids' Clubs Network *and* TECs.

Maternity Alliance
45 Beech Street, London EC2P 2LX
0171 588 8582 (advice line)
Works for improvement in health care, social and financial support for parents-to-be, mothers, fathers and babies in the first year of life. A good source of information on statutory maternity and parental rights, leave and pay.

Meet-A-Mum Association (MAMA)
14 Willis Road, Croydon CRO 2XX
0181 665 0357
0181 656 7318 (helpline)
Provides support and counselling to mothers suffering from post-natal depression and those with young children. Runs daytime social meetings, evening meetings with speakers, babysitting and 'mother-to-mother' support for those who are feeling lonely, isolated or depressed.

Montessori St Nicholas Centre
23–24 Princes Gate, London SW7 1PT
0171 225 1277
For information on the Montessori method and philosophy of early years' education.

National Association for Maternal and Child Welfare
1st Floor, 40–42 Osnaburgh Street, London NW1 3ND
0171 383 4117
For information on content of child care training syllabuses.

National Association of Citizen's Advice Bureaux
115–123 Pentonville Road, London N1 9LZ.
0171 833 2181
For information on local citizens' advice bureaux.

National Association of Nursery Nurses
10 Meriden Court, Great Clacton, Essex CO15 4XH
01255 476707
A national organisation of local branches where nursery nurses regularly meet to share professional practice of child care and early education. May be a 'nanny finding' source.

National Childbirth Trust
Alexandra House, Oldham Terrace, London W3 6NH
0181 992 8637
Has 400 branches around the UK. Provides antenatal classes, breast-feeding counselling and postnatal support. Runs special support groups for parents with disabilities and for those who have miscarried.

National Childminding Association (NCMA)
8 Mason's Hill, Bromley, Kent BR2 9EY
0181 466 0200 (advice line)
A membership organisation for childminders. Aims to raise the status and standards of childminding. Provides advice, information and a network of local support groups. May be able to put parents in touch with local childminders.

National Children's Bureau
8 Wakley Street, London EC1V 7QE
0171 843 6000
A national organisation concerned with children's needs in the family, school and society. Excellent resource library. Undertakes research, policy and practice development. Services Parliamentary Group for Children.

National Council for One Parent Families
255 Kentish Town Road, London NW5 2LX
0171 267 1361
Campaigns to improve the economic, legal and social position of one-parent families. Offers re-employment training and an information service for single parents. Also publishes a number of publications including a guide to holidays.

National Council for Vocational Qualifications (NVQs)
222 Euston Road, London NW1 2BZ
0171 387 9898
The accrediting body for all NVQs in England, Wales and Northern Ireland. Responsible for quality, assuring the work of awarding bodies, including those on child care.

National Early Years Network
77 Holloway Road, London N7 8JZ
0171 607 9573
Provides practical support to all those working with young children. Publishes information leaflets for parents on Choosing Childcare, Getting the Safety Habit, *and a guide to tackling discrimination in child care* Playing Fair?

National Stepfamily Association
Chapel Street, 18 Hatton Place, London EC1N 8JH
0171 209 2460
Offers telephone counselling service and runs local self-help groups.

New Ways to Work
309 Upper Street, London N1 2TY
0171 226 4026
Promotes new approaches to the time patterns of work. Answers enquiries from individuals, researchers, trade unions and employers. Encourages equal access to jobs for people who have caring and domestic responsibilities and for people with disabilities.

Norland College
Denford Park, Hungerford, Berkshire RG17 0PQ
01488 682252
Provides training in the care and education of children under eight. Has its own international employment agency for Norland qualified nannies. Offers on-site facilities for local children including a nursery school, day care units, the Norland Children's Hotel (24-hour care), after-school and holiday care, and activity weekends.

Opportunity 2000
44 Baker Street, London WC1H 1DH
0171 224 1600
Set up in 1991 to increase the quality and quantity of women's participation in the workplace at all levels, based on ability. A good source of advice for family friendly business arguments.

The Parent Network
Room 2, Winchester House, 11 Cranmer Road,
London SW9 6EJ
0171 735 1214
Provides support and education for parents (known as Parent-Link) in their local communities aimed at helping parents and children feel better about themselves and each other.

Parents At Work
45 Beech Street, London EC2Y 8AD
0171 628 3565
An organisation committed to the welfare of children of working parents, Parents At Work works with employers with the aim of introducing 'quality of life' conditions into the workplace which benefit both employers and employees. A membership-based organisation, it operates a network of support groups and links working parents of special needs children with others in their area.

Pre-school Learning Alliance (PLA)
69 King's Cross Road, London WC1X 9LL
0171 833 0991
Represents a range of pre-school groups including: sessional play groups, parent and toddler groups, under-fives play groups, opportunity play groups, family centres, extended day care and full-day play groups/nurseries for children under five.

Professional Association of Nursery Nurses (PANN)
2 St James' Court, Friar Gate, Derby DE1 1BT
01332 343029
Membership of PANN (for nursery nurses and qualified nannies) includes insurance against action brought by employers, legal advice and personal representation. PANN operates a strict 'no strike' rule.

Public Concern at Work
Lincoln's Inn House, 42 Kingsway, London WC2B 6EN
0171 404 6609
Provides free legal advice, especially to employees, who are worried about malpractice at work.

Relate
Herbert Gray College, Little Church Street, Rugby,
Warwickshire CV21 3AP
01788 573241
Co-ordinates approximately 130 local Relate centres around the UK which provide couple counselling for those with relationship problems.

Rights of Women
52–54 Featherstone Street, London EC1Y 8RT
0171 251 6577 – various times
Informs women of their legal rights. Offers free telephone advice.

Scottish Childminding Association
Room 7, Stirling Business Centre, Wellgreen, Stirling SK8 2DZ
01786 445377
See also NCMA.

Scottish Out of School Care Network
55 Renfrew Street, Glasgow G2 3BD
0141 331 1301
See also Kids' Clubs Network.

Scottish Pre-school Play Association
SPPA Centre, 14 Elliot Place, Glasgow G3 8EP
0141 221 4148
See also PLA.

Single Parent Links and Special Holidays (SPLASH)
19 North Street, Plymouth, Devon PL4 9AH
01752 674067
Provides holidays for single-parent families, with some reductions for families on low incomes. Also offers children-only holidays during the summer holidays.

St John Ambulance
1 Grosvenor Crescent, London SW1X 7EF
0171 235 5231
For information on first aid training, for adults and children.

Steiner Waldorf Schools Fellowship
Kidbrooke Park, Forest Row, East Sussex RH18 5JB
01342 822115

Stillbirth and Neonatal Death Society (SANDS)
28 Portland Place, London W1N 4DE
0171 436 7940

TECs (Training and Enterprise Councils) National Council
Westminster Tower, 3 Albert Embankment, London SE1 7SX
0171 735 0010
*For details of local Training and Enterprise Councils in England
and Wales, and for information on training/career development
grants and child care.*
See also LECs *and* Kids' Clubs Network.

TUC (Trades Union Congress)
Congress House, Great Russell Street, London WC1
0171 6364030
*For information and advice on statutory employment rights and
benefits. Ask for Equal Rights Unit.*

Twins and Multiple Births Association (TAMBA)
PO Box 30, Little Sutton, South Wirral L66 1TH
0151 348 0020
01732 868000 (helpline)
*Exists to give encouragement and support to parents of twins,
triplets or other multiple births. TAMBA runs a network of support groups throughout the UK. It also maintains specialist
groups for bereaved parents, for one-parent families and for
families with special needs.*

Wales Pre-school Playgroups Association
2a Chester Street, Wrexham, Clwyd LL13 8BD
01978 358195
See also PLA.

Women Returners' Network
8 John Adam Street, London WC2N 6EZ
0171 839 8188
Promotes education, training and employment opportunities that meet the needs of women, to facilitate their return to the workforce. Offers information and guidance.

Working For Childcare
77 Holloway Road, London N7 8JZ
0171 700 0281
Encourages the development of child care facilities to meet the needs of working parents and the social, educational and welfare requirements of their children. Promotes the development of all work-related child care.

Index